# My Mother's Bolivian Kitchen

## Recipes and Recollections

# The Hippocrene Cookbook Library

Afghan Food & Cookery
African Cooking, Best of Regional
Albanian Cooking, Best of
Alps, Cuisines of The
Aprovecho: A Mexican-American Border
  Cookbook
Argentina Cooks!, Exp. Ed.
Austrian Cuisine, Best of, Exp. Ed.
Brazilian Cookery, The Art of
Bulgarian Cooking, Traditional
Burma, Flavors of
Cajun Women, Cooking with
Calabria, Cucina di
Caucasus Mountains, Cuisines of the
Chile, Tasting
Colombian Cooking, Secrets of
Croatian Cooking, Best of, Exp. Ed.
Czech Cooking, Best of, Exp. Ed.
Danube, All Along The, Exp. Ed.
Dutch Cooking, Art of, Exp. Ed.
Egyptian Cooking
Filipino Food, Fine
Finnish Cooking, Best of
French Caribbean Cuisine
French Fashion, Cooking in the
  (Bilingual)
Germany, Spoonfuls of
Greek Cuisine, The Best of, Exp. Ed.
Gypsy Feast
Haiti, Taste of
Havana Cookbook, Old (Bilingual)
Hungarian Cookbook
Hungarian Cooking, Art of, Rev. Ed.
Icelandic Food & Cookery
India, Flavorful
Indian Spice Kitchen
International Dictionary of
  Gastronomy
Irish-Style, Feasting Galore
Italian Cuisine, Treasury of (Bilingual)
Japanese Home Cooking
Korean Cuisine, Best of
Laotian Cooking, Simple

Latvia, Taste of
Lithuanian Cooking, Art of
Macau, Taste of
Middle Eastern Kitchen, The
Mongolian Cooking, Imperial
New Hampshire: from Farm to Kitchen
Norway, Tastes and Tales of
Persian Cooking, Art of
Poland's Gourmet Cuisine
Polish Cooking, Best of, Exp. Ed.
Polish Country Kitchen Cookbook
Polish Cuisine, Treasury of (Bilingual)
Polish Heritage Cookery, Ill. Ed.
Polish Traditions, Old
Portuguese Encounters, Cuisines of
Pyrenees, Tastes of
Quebec, Taste of
Rhine, All Along The
Romania, Taste of, Exp. Ed.
Russian Cooking, Best of, Exp. Ed.
Scandinavian Cooking, Best of
Scotland, Traditional Food From
Scottish-Irish Pub and Hearth
  Cookbook
Sephardic Israeli Cuisine
Sicilian Feasts
Slovak Cooking, Best of
Smorgasbord Cooking, Best of
South African Cookery, Traditional
South American Cookery, Art of
South Indian Cooking, Healthy
Spanish Family Cookbook, Rev. Ed.
Sri Lanka, Exotic Tastes of
Swedish Kitchen
Swiss Cookbook, The
Syria, Taste of
Taiwanese Cuisine, Best of
Thai Cuisine, Best of, Regional
Turkish Cuisine, Taste of
Ukrainian Cuisine, Best of, Exp. Ed.
Uzbek Cooking, Art of
Warsaw Cookbook, Old

# My Mother's Bolivian Kitchen

## Recipes and Recollections

José Sánchez-H.

HIPPOCRENE BOOKS
NEW YORK

Book and jacket design by Acme Klong Design, Inc.
Food photography by José Sánchez-H.
Illustrations by Domenic Cretara.

For more information, address:
HIPPOCRENE BOOKS, INC.
171 Madison Avenue
New York, NY 10016

ISBN 0-7818-1056-6
Cataloging-in-Publication Data available from the Library of Congress.
Printed in the United States of America.

*To Tina, Guichy, Carla and Mary*

# CONTENTS

# ACKNOWLEDGMENTS

I am grateful to my wife Tina for her vision in suggesting I write down the stories of my childhood and combine them with recipes. Her persistence and encouragement for me to send a book proposal to a publisher, after reading the *Todos Santos* memoir, made this publication a reality. Her unwavering editorial help in the writing of the manuscript is deeply appreciated.

The other person who made this book a reality is Anne McBride, former editor-in-chief of Hippocrene Books, Inc. I owe her my gratitude for her editorial work and helpful suggestions, as well as for her guidance and continuous support during times when I needed it the most. Because of my teaching schedule, I could mainly work on this book during summertime, and Anne never gave up on me.

Many thanks to Rebecca Cole, my current editor at Hippocrene Books, Inc., who took over this project and guided it to completion. Her attention to detail and valuable suggestions were very helpful for me to complete this book.

Katareya Wilson Godehn made excellent use of the artwork and created a beautiful design for this book. Iris Bass, my copyeditor, did a wonderful job in the early revisions of the manuscript.

I am thankful to my sisters Guichy, Carla, and Mary, and my niece Gina for providing me with Bolivian recipes for this book, and to my family in Bolivia for always feeding me so well when I visit. Thanks also to Jorge, Carlita, Pablo, Verónica, Félix, Daniela, Favi, Miguel, Paola, and Efro. And to Justina and Apolonia for their great cooking.

My appreciation and gratitude to the family of my mentor and teacher Alejandro Gómez and his family for taking such a good care of me when I lived in Mexico. His parents Josefina and Luis, grandmothers Lupita and Nina, sisters and brothers, Amparo, Magdalena, Teresa, Carmen, Angeles, Gabriel, José, Ignacio, José Luis, Adalberto, and all the Mexican families that adopted me and fed me.

My gratitude to Joseph and Doris, who not only enjoy my cooking, but who always provide their love and support. To Chuck and Paula for sharing their joy in making memories with family, appreciating the value of homemade food, and at times working together in the kitchen making yucca with cheese. To Hannah, Claire, Cynthia, Joseph, Stephen, Carolyn, Deanna, Gabor, Rob, Kathy, David, Jonathan and Jim.

To Rudi for his interest in my work throughout these years and who, at the age of 100, continues to be a major inspiration.

Many thanks to Fred Sr., Margaret, Susan, Fred Jr., Cynthia, Alex, Robin and Caroline.

Domenic Cretara agreed to do the illustrations for this book and I am thankful for his artistic input, which I value highly from having worked with him on other creative projects as well. His sensitivity as an artist makes this more than a cookbook. Thanks also to Betty and the Cretara family.

Finally, my thanks to California State University, Long Beach for my position as professor which afforded me time in the summers to write a memoir about food. My gratitude to Robert C. Maxson, Douglas Robinson, Armando Contreras, Donald J. Para, Craig Smith, and Sharyn C. Blumenthal for their continuous support of my scholarly and creative work.

I am thankful to Robert Freligh for his valuable help creating digital photographic files of old negatives that belonged to my father, which were used as a source for the illustrations of this book. Domenic Cretara created original work for the "La Carne" memoir. The "Tinku" illustrations are based on a photographs by Oscar E. Ruiz Calero; the illustration for "A Trip to the Mountains," is based on a photograph taken by my sister Carla Sánchez de Rocha, who ventured to travel with me on my motorcycle on many occasions.

# FOREWORD

The smell of food, any type of food, brings back memories of my childhood, and with those memories the aromas of many dishes made in my mother's kitchen. I wrote this book to keep her memory alive, as well as to deal somehow with her departure from life. My mother's life and cooking were denied to me forever by the irresponsibility of a drunk driver, who hit the car she was riding in on Easter day in 1998.

As with many people who leave home, there are moments when we miss the people we love and very often the meals that we ate with them. Bolivian food is not as well known or available in the U.S. as perhaps Chinese, Italian or Mexican food, which in my college days made the longing for the food of my country even greater. There were no places I could go to have the dishes I grew up eating. Perhaps one of the best gifts I got from my mother is a love of cooking, because it allowed me to eat real food rather than gulp endless variations of burgers during my college years overseas, which was the case with most of my friends.

I started to cook as a child by observing my mother in her kitchen while I listened to the stories she told me. I never really did a complete job of cooking then. It was mostly keeping an eye on things, like making sure the food didn't burn or the soup didn't spill, peeling potatoes or cutting vegetables. Perhaps the only full task I had back then in my mother's kitchen was boiling water with cocoa bean skins or another herbal tea we were having for teatime.

When I left home at the age of eighteen, I began—out of necessity—to connect with my feminine side. I realized then that in order to eat some of the delicious dishes prepared by my mother, I had to develop any cooking skills I possessed or had inherited from her. It wasn't until I was in my forties that I began to grasp what my mother felt when she let her only son go far away from her cooking and loving care. My experiences have helped me understand the sacrifices my parents made in order for me to have a better life. I saw my parents and three sisters as often as I could after my departure from Bolivia, but never returned to live there due to the circumstances of my education and professional life.

Cooking became a form of communion with the family I left behind in Bolivia. I started by making the dishes I missed the most, like the daily soups I couldn't find on the menus in any of the countries I lived in—Mexico, the U.S., Puerto Rico, and Spain. In the Caribbean I made all kinds of soups for my friends. In Mexico I introduced *humintas* (corn dumplings) for teatime, something new but very much welcomed as a tradition by my friends there.

The eating schedule in Bolivia starts with breakfast early in the morning, which can include a variety of natural teas like *cacao*, *sultana*, *cedrón*, *manzanilla*, or for some coffee or *api*. This is accompanied by bread, or sometimes cheese-filled *pasteles*. Around 10 a.m. there is a mid-morning snack of *salteñas* and a soda. *Salteñas* are similar to empanadas, filled with chicken or beef, vegetables, eggs, and raisins. The Bolivian lunch always consists of a *primero*, usually soup, and a *segundo* which is normally a poultry or meat dish. There is peanut soup, potato soup, and pumpkin soup, among many others. In the afternoon at 4 p.m. tea is served religiously in every home or office, often accompanied by cheese empanadas or some type of sweet bread. This Bolivian tradition came from the British when they were building the railroads in South America. Around 7 p.m. dinner is served and can be anything from *sill'panchu* (breaded beef cutlets) to a *picante de pollo* (spicy chicken) or some other dish. Before going to sleep, people may drink coca tea to help with the altitude, as the city of La Paz is 12,000 feet above sea level.

When I lived in Mexico, because of the different eating schedule and the absence of teatime, my stomach would go into spasms of hunger. In Mexico, they usually eat a big lunch around 2 p.m., but do not have tea in the afternoon. No matter how much I ate for lunch, it seemed my stomach retained an empty space for tea that cried for attention. However, as time went by, that space was abandoned and soon forgotten amidst the demands of life and the cultural differences I adapted to and lived with.

Eventually the teatime ritual disappeared, much like the birthday I used to await with so much excitement when I was a child. My father would tell me the story of the "Chinese" who came back from a trip with something for me. The "Chinese" was a beautiful empty glass bottle shaped like a Chinese man that my father filled up with cookies and candy for my birthday. It was such a thrilling experience to open that bottle on my birthday, that on those days I awoke early without my mother having to wake me like on other days for school. My birthdays later became like any other day, where work takes priority and magic is forgotten. For years I let the day remain like the empty Chinese bottle waiting for cookies and candy.

However, in recent times, my wife and I have adopted the ritual of drinking tea at 4 p.m. when we are together. And I now make my own empanadas. Drinking tea gives continuity to my life because of the skill and gift of cooking I kept with me all these years. I take it wherever I go and, with it, my mother's kitchen.

# BOLIVIA

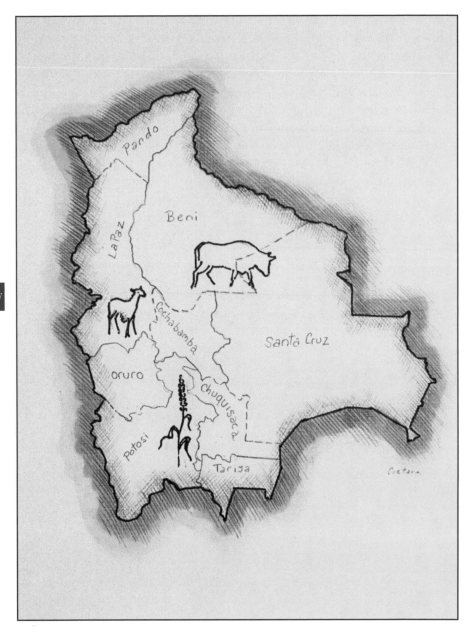

# A LOOK INTO BOLIVIA

Bolivia lies in the heart of South America, surrounded by
Brazil, Peru, Paraguay, Argentina, and Chile. Approximately the size of
California and Texas together, in 2003 Bolivia had an estimated popula-
tion of 8,586,000. Its administrative capital, La Paz, (the legal capital is
Sucre) is the highest capital city in the world (11,900 feet) and is located
near Lake Titicaca, the world's highest navigable lake (12,500 feet).

The earliest civilization in Bolivia, the Tiahuanaco kingdom, was established around Lake Titicaca in 600 B.C. It was conquered by the Incas in
the thirteenth century, who were in turn conquered by the Spanish in the
sixteenth century. The Incas were pushed off of their lands and exploited
by the Spanish. Forced to pay massive tributes, they worked under inhu-
mane conditions and died by the thousands at the silver mines of Potosi.
They did fight back, however, and were a constant source of opposition to
the Spanish authorities. There were a number of Indian uprisings before
and after Bolivia gained its independence from Spain in 1825.

Not counting what was smuggled, the Spanish crown took 16,000 tons
of silver (16 million kilograms) between 1546 and 1660. This amount
represents three and a half times the entire European reserves of the day.
All of this did not remain in Spain, however. Much of it was spent to
finance the country's religious wars. Ultimately, German, English, and
Flemish bankers ended up with much of the wealth taken from the once
"Rich Hill of Potosi." This wealth later financed the industrial development of northern Europe.

## OVERVIEW OF POLITICAL HISTORY

Bolivia's history since its liberation from Spanish rule has been marked by
recurrent disorder and instability. Weak governments have made the
country defenseless against the appropriation of its territory by its neighbors. Chile invaded Bolivia in 1879 in an altercation over minerals and
guano, and annexed Bolivian coastal areas along the Pacific Ocean. The
Pacific War (1879–83) with Chile left Bolivia without access to the sea or

its rich nitrate fields. In 1903, Bolivia lost its largest rubber-producing regions to Brazil. The Chaco Wars with Paraguay (1928–30 and 1933–35) also brought great losses of life and territory. Other losses of territory resulted from treaties with Argentina, Brazil, and Peru.

Bolivia's political history has been so complex and turbulent that it is not possible to do it justice in the space available here. As with many developing nations, its history has been characterized by economic domination by foreign interests and political domination by authoritarian governments that support the concentration of power in the hands of a small, elite group. The following is a brief summary of events that highlight Bolivia's political history from the 1950s to the present.

## THE REVOLUTION OF 1952

Growing unrest in the mid-twentieth century culminated in the 1952 revolution. The resulting government under Victor Paz Estenssoro nationalized the mines and instituted the first major agrarian reform in Latin America since the Mexican Revolution. Leader of the revolution, Paz Estenssoro held the Bolivian presidency in 1952–56, 1960–64, and 1985–1989.

In 1961, Bolivia, like most Latin American countries, shifted toward an alignment with the United States. This move led to the Alliance for Progress, initiated by President John F. Kennedy in 1961 in an attempt to establish economic cooperation between the countries of Latin America and the U.S. The Alliance for Progress was also a reaction to communist Cuba. The U.S. feared that communism would spread throughout the region. Thus, democratic governments and tax and land reform were conditions for U.S. aid. However, the Alliance for Progress ended in 1973 when most Latin American nations no longer embraced it.

## THE RISE OF MILITARY REGIMES

In 1964, Paz Estenssoro was overthrown by General René Barrientos Ortuño, then vice president. That year, Bolivia became one of the first countries in the region to move from a democratic civilian government to an authoritarian military government, a trend that spread throughout Latin America. The National Security Doctrine, initiated under the government of U.S. President Lyndon B. Johnson, like the Alliance for Progress, had a strong anticommunist sentiment. The armed forces in Bolivia, as in the rest of Latin America, were strengthened under right-wing military governments and had the unrestricted support of the U.S. Authoritarian rule generated repressive governments with no respect for human rights and with an obsessive anticommunist attitude. As a result, Bolivia experienced a series of violent confrontations between the army and the left.

In 1965, General Barrientos Ortuño faced strong opposition to his government from the country's miners. A gathering of miners in the town of Catavi ended in a massacre ordered by his military regime.

In October 1967, the guerrilla uprising led by Argentine revolutionary Ernesto "Ché" Guevara had a tragic ending. Guevara had played an important role in the Cuban revolution. His capture in Bolivia resulted in his execution by a U.S.-backed military delegation working in conjunction with the military government of General Barrientos Ortuño.

In 1969, after the general's death in a helicopter crash, a series of back-to-back military coups began in Bolivia and continued throughout the 1970s, in response to widespread strikes, disorder, and political unrest.

From 1971 to 1978, during the military regime of Colonel (later General) Hugo Bánzer Suárez, all political and union activities were banned.

In 1979, the crimson coup of Colonel Alberto Natusch Busch replaced the short-lived government of civilian interim president Walter Guevara Arze. Also that year the first Bolivian woman president, Lidia Gueiler Tejada, was appointed by the Bolivian National Congress.

In 1980, a coup by General Luis García Meza interrupted the Congress' selection of Hernán Siles Zuazo for the presidency. Klaus Barbie, the former Gestapo chief in the town of Lyon, France, known as the "Butcher of Lyon" and responsible for the death of thousands of Jews, directed this bloody coup, which led to torture, disappearances, arrests, and the production and trafficking of cocaine. On October 25, 1982, *Newsweek* magazine published an article entitled "The Civilians Take Charge," which mentioned that Klaus Barbie had been among the Argentine and Austro-German neo-Nazis who had worked as paramilitaries for the García Meza regime under Minister of the Interior Colonel Luis Arce Gómez.

A military uprising forced the right-wing military government under General Luis García Meza to resign in August 1981. General García Meza's credibility had been badly damaged by the army's involvement in the cocaine trade, by the economic crisis and default on Bolivia's foreign debt, and by continuing labor and political unrest.

# THE RETURN OF CIVILIAN GOVERNMENT

President General Guido Vildoso Calderón handed the presidency back to Congress in 1982 after being in power less than a year. The military regime of General Vildoso Calderón couldn't resolve the badly damaged economy nor the discontent of a people whose frustrations had transformed into constant strikes. In 1982, Bolivia returned to civilian rule when Congress elected Hernán Siles Zuazo as president.

Siles Zuazo was a leader of the center-left Movimiento Nacionalista Revolucionario (MNR) that presided over the 1952 revolution and ruled Bolivia from 1952–64. After three years as president, government spending and the devaluation of the Bolivian peso brought the exchange rate to two hundred pesos per dollar.

In June 1984, President Siles Zuazo was briefly abducted by several right-wing military officers, an event that brought turmoil to the country. The same year, a right-wing plot to overthrow him, in addition to strikes and political unrest, ended in his call for new elections. The devaluation of the peso reached nine thousand pesos per dollar.

The result of the August 1985 election marked Victor Paz Estenssoro's third return to power under difficult circumstances. In 1985, inflation reached fifty thousand pesos per dollar and the country demanded immediate action toward resolving this economic crisis.

Paz Estenssoro's goal was to stabilize the Bolivian currency and put an end to hyperinflation, with a new decree known as 21060. This was achieved in record time, dropping from 8,767 percent in 1985 to 16 percent in 1989. However, the measures taken by the Paz Estenssoro government to stop inflation seemed too austere to the trade union Central Obrera Boliviana (COB), which called a strike lasting fifteen days. Other demonstrations against the Paz Estenssoro government resulted in detentions and a three-month state of siege.

In 1986, the Paz Estenssoro government also experienced strong criticism from opposition groups and trade unions, for allowing U.S. soldiers, in collaboration with the Bolivian army, to destroy coca plantations.

Following another election, President Jaime Paz Zamora governed from 1989 to 1993. Paz Zamora resorted to diplomatic means with the international community in a campaign defending coca leaf production. Called "Coca for Development," the campaign showed various positive uses for coca leaves and tried to differentiate these from illegal trafficking. When Spanish authorities opposed the exhibition of coca leaves and coca tea at Expo-Sevilla '92, the former ambassador of Bolivia to Spain, Fernando Cajias, stated that "Coca is not cocaine, just as grapes are not wine."

The second Summit of Heads of State of Iberoamerican countries in Spain marked the beginning of an informative campaign about the medicinal and nutritional uses of coca leaves. As a result, requests for scientific studies were presented to the World Health Organization with support from the governments of Spain and Germany.

During his term, President Paz Zamora met twice with President George H. W. Bush to discuss the issue of the coca farming in Bolivia. In both meetings, the emphasis on repression was maintained, but the need for an alternative option was also recognized. Information about the presidents' mutual decision to militarize the fight against narcotics was not released. When this information came out, there was strong opposition and criticism in Bolivia.

The political debates that occurred during elections in 1993 represent a significant advance in Bolivia's troubled political history. This type of televised debate, conducted by the well-respected historian, film critic/producer and current president of Bolivia, Carlos D. Mesa Gisbert, was unheard of during the military regimes. The elected president was another civilian, Gonzalo Sánchez de Lozada, who defeated former military dictator General Hugo Banzer Suárez. Sánchez de Lozada, a successful businessman and a former film producer, produced *Mina Alaska* (1968) by Jorge Ruiz, the first Latin American film to be restored by the Academy of Motion Picture Arts and Sciences Film Archive in the year 2002. His changes to the education system in Bolivia were lauded at the State of the World Forum in Guanajuato, Mexico in 1996.

In 1995, there was strong economic pressure from the U.S. government to destroy 5,400 hectares of coca under threat of political and economic embargo and the blocking of credit from the International Development Bank. The minister of government, Carlos Sánchez Berzaín, confirmed that more than 5,520 hectares of coca worth 13.8 million dollars had been destroyed in order to meet the U.S. demands.

One of the most dramatic events in 1995 was the Marcha de las Cocaleras, the march of Bolivian women coca farmers. Around two hundred peasant women from the region of Chapare gathered on December 18, 1995, in the Plaza 14 de Septiembre in the city of Cochabamba. Challenged by mountainous paths, snow, and lack of shelter, they walked more than 370 miles (600 kilometers), with their children, toward La Paz. Their goal was to meet President Sánchez de Lozada and request an end to the forced destruction of coca, freedom for the detained peasants, development of alternative agricultural crops, and respect for life.

Also in 1995, General Luis García Meza became the only Latin American former dictator to serve a jail sentence for human rights abuses, murder, drug trafficking charges, and misuse of funds. He was captured in 1995 in Brazil and is currently serving a thirty-year sentence in the Chonchoro jail of La Paz.

In 1997, the disputed election of General Hugo Bánzer Suárez to the presidency received mixed reactions in a country where the return to military government was again met with strong opposition from the workers.

In 2002, Gonzalo Sánchez de Lozada was elected for a second term. However, in 2003 after only fourteen months in the presidency, Sánchez de Lozada faced riots and opposition to his plans to boost the economy in Bolivia. His proposal to export natural gas to the U.S. and Mexico through a port in Chile instead of Peru generated opposition that led to the deaths of Indian and labor leaders. The resentment over having lost its coastal territory to Chile when Bolivia was invaded during the Pacific War (1879-83) remains an issue in this landlocked country. As a result of this opposition, Sánchez de Lozada was forced to resign. He left the country for the U.S. and Vice President Mesa Gisbert became president.

# 6 TYPICAL FOODS

Bolivia, once part of the Inca Empire, was called Alto Peru by the Spanish. The Inca language, Quechua, is still spoken, as well as the Aymara language. Bolivian cuisine reflects the influence of these indigenous cultures, as well as the Spanish culture. The Incas had large domesticated mammals, including the llama and alpaca, which could transport food in the high regions of the Andes. They also consumed animals like deer, guinea pig, and *guanaco* (a llama-like animal). The Inca culture was advanced in the domestication of plants. Bolivia's geographical position in the Andes Mountains makes for a high number of micro-climates. Maize was one of the principal crops along with quinoa and potatoes. The sophisticated preservation methods used by the Incas such freeze-drying potatoes continue to be used today in the Andean regions of Bolivia.

There are 1,290 kinds of potatoes in Bolivia, and Bolivians are the biggest potato consumers in the world. Seven of the nine states in Bolivia produce potatoes. The variety of climates—from Andean mountains and valleys to the Amazon jungle—gives Bolivia enormous biological diversity. Being accustomed to this diversity led to my greatest challenge when I moved overseas, for example, when it came to preparing dishes that required certain types of potatoes, like *papalisa* that are not available in the U.S. This small potato, its flesh yellow with pink, red, or green dots, is great in soups and other dishes. *Papalisas* are grown in Cochabamba, Oruro, Potosi, Sucre, and Tarija. There are two hundred varieties of these small yellow tubers, which are also known as *ullucu* or *melloco*. They are said to be rich in vitamins and minerals.

Another floury tuber known as *oca* is worth trying. The states where you are likely to find this exotic tuber are Cochabamba, La Paz, Oruro, Sucre, and Tarija. It comes in various colors, such as yellow, black, and red. The Bolivians sun-dry *oca* for days before cooking it, so it becomes much sweeter. It can be boiled or baked, and is served with a variety of meat dishes and salads.

The food in Bolivia changes throughout the country depending on which crops can be grown in each region. The mountain states, La Paz, Oruro, and Potosi, tend to use more starches, such as potatoes, rice, and quinoa. The fertile valley states, Cochabamba, Sucre, and Tarija, feature more vegetables and fruits. Fish from rivers and lakes are also an important part of their diet. The valley regions also produce a good variety of potatoes and *oca*, and use rice in their meals. Most food is served with a hot sauce, known by the Quechua word *uchu llajwa*, which is made from a small hot pepper called *locoto*. The sauce normally contains tomatoes, *locotos*, salt, and an aromatic herb known as *quilquiña*. In the U.S., this hot sauce can be made using cilantro in place of the *quilquiña*.

In Pando, Beni, and Santa Cruz, which are in the Amazon basin, potatoes are replaced by yucca and plantains. The use of rice in this region is also predominant.

It is customary to eat some form of protein at lunch and dinner. Fish, such as trout can be found in Lake Titicaca, and then there is the tasty *surubi* fish found in the Amazon region. Lamb and goat are common in the Altiplano. Pork is popular throughout Bolivia and is usually part of the Sunday menu. In the valley regions it is served in the traditional *chicharronerias*, restaurants serving pork cracklings.

Throughout the world, festivals and celebrations call for the preparation of special meals, and Bolivian culture is no exception. The most celebrated feasts are Christmas Day and New Year's Eve, when the meal usually includes pork, turkey or duck. Carnival is characterized by a sweet known as *confite*, as well as dishes like *puchero de carnaval*. Holy Week is a time for *papalisa* dishes because the *papalisa* tuber is in season, as well as the consumption of fish dishes. Mother's Day, which in Bolivia is always on May 27, features meat or a special soup. A special meal, including such dishes as roast pork or a *picante de lengua* are prepared for Independence Day on August 6, and enjoyed among friends and family. The November Empanada Feast in Sucre offers a great display of baked goods including *salteñas*. The potato festival on April 4 and 5 in the village of Betanzos, Potosi includes a good display of folk music and Bolivian dances, in addition to a wide array of potato dishes.

Drinking tea is a common Bolivian custom. One of the most popular teas found in restaurants and markets is *trimate*, a blend of chamomile, aniseed, and coca. There is also plain coca tea. The coca plant has been used in Bolivia for centuries for medicinal and nutritional purposes. Coca tea is especially helpful for preventing and alleviating symptoms of altitude sickness.

Among the alcoholic drinks found in Bolivia, the most popular is the fermented corn beverage, *chicha*. This preferred drink of the masses is usually sold in *chicherias*, which are easy to spot because they have small white banners posted outside. The best *chicha* is made in the valley state of Cochabamba. *Chicha* is made from both yellow and red corn. The one made from red corn is called *chicha kulli*, or red *chicha*, and the other one is referred to as *chicha*. Beer is another popular drink—some of the breweries in Bolivia were established by German immigrants. Beer is brewed in several states: Taquiña in Cochabamba, Paceña and Pilsener in La Paz, and Sureña in the state of Sucre. Although you probably won't find Bolivian wine in U.S. stores, wines produced in the state of Tarija are quite good and very inexpensive. Pisco, singani and guarapo are other popular grape liquors.

The chocolate made in Sucre has a reputation of being as good, if not better than some of the best chocolate in Switzerland. One of the sweets found in Bolivia during Carnival season is *confite*, which is boiled sugar syrup filled with nuts, roasted peas, or fruit. *Confite* comes in different sizes and has a round shape. It is also used in *cha'lla*, a word describing any ritual blessing, including the festivities that pay tribute to Mother Earth. The *cha'lla* can be applied to a house or even a car.

One of the challenges of cooking Bolivian food in the U.S. can be finding unusual ingredients, like the white corn needed to make *humintas*, or *quesillo* cheese. However, you may find some ingredients at a Mexican market, and others can be replaced with more readily available ingredients. If all else fails there is the internet, where these days you may find any of the ingredients needed for Bolivian cooking (www.bolivianmall.com).

# TINKU

As I descend from the truck that took us along the Caine River in northern Potosi, I fall into my father's arms and am lowered to the ground. He is wearing his brown poncho this morning.

The poncho my father wore for traveling to the countryside was as thick as the Bolivian blankets, which are made of wool and are quite heavy—especially to a five-year-old. I couldn't move much in bed if I had two or three of these blankets to protect me from the cold weather, and so I called my father's poncho the blanket poncho. It had a neck like a regular shirt, and was two shades of brown, one darker and one lighter with white. The design had small squares like a chessboard, although this time the game was traveling. That piece of wool was woven into my life, and many years later brought good memories, when I would lie on my bed using the poncho as a blanket, and be covered by its warmth. It was like being covered by time and protected by the person who was no longer in my life, my father.

I watch my father collect our luggage, two leather suitcases the color of time—brown. The Caine River greets us with its passing noise, its water colored by red clay that the rain had washed from the soil. I hear my mother saying, "There he is!"

From the other side of the river, a voice calls, "Victor! Margarita!" It is my uncle Zenón, sitting on a muscular brown horse on the other side of the river with two black horses beside him. My parents and I watch him cross the river as he pulls the horses along, behind him. As the brown horse he rides cuts through the water, the river reaches the horse's knees.

Zenón is in his late forties with big dark eyes, dark brown hair, a light complexion, and a friendly smile. When he reaches our side of the river, he bends over to greet me, saying "Hi, traveler!"

I excitedly greet him with a question: "Hi, Uncle Zenón, did you bring food?"

He laughs and tells me that first we have to cross the river on the horses and that the food is at the other side of the river. After crossing the Caine River, we eat hot purple potatoes, *quesillo*, and beef cooked in a sauce with fava beans. The food is in a clay pot wrapped in a colorful *aguayo* (wool weaving) to keep it warm. When it is unwrapped and the lid is lifted, the smell of the fava beans, meat, potatoes, and cheese steams out like a genie. The smell of food is as strong as my hunger. Other scents from that day also remain imbedded in my memory: the smell of the red-clay colored river roaring like an excited animal and the smell of horse-shit. The wind blends all these scents together in the air, forming the smell of Bolivian countryside.

Later, I ride behind my father, holding tight to his poncho. The horse's hoofbeats seem in rhythm with the scenery of the mountains and the valley that my eyes glimpse along our way. To our right, my mother and my uncle Zenón ride their horses. As I watch them talking, my head moves up and down because of the trot of the horse. The next day, in the early afternoon, we arrive at the town of Toro-Toro, and my small behind is sore from the journey.

After spending some time that day talking with my parents and Uncle Zenón and listening to their conversation, I venture into the kitchen to look for a carrot to eat. *Zanahorita* is the Spanish word for "little carrot." Somehow, when I was five years old, I had difficulty saying that word. No matter how hard I tried to say it right, it always came out as if I was saying *señorita*, "miss" in Spanish. When I ask for a little carrot, a woman in the kitchen tells me there are no *"señoritas"* in the kitchen. She also mentions that she hasn't been to the market yet, as a way of saying she is busy. I wonder if she knows I want a little carrot or if she is just too busy to be dealing with a five-year-old. People in this town went to the market every day to buy their vegetables, because they wanted to have fresh produce.

From the patio, I see the big wooden door of the house standing open. I decide to go out, to look for a carrot in the market. As my feet carry me outside the walls of my uncle's house, I see some peasants and Indian women passing me as if I don't exist. They are hurrying toward a clamor of voices coming from somewhere in the distance. I follow them, since I figure they probably know where I can find a carrot. When I ask them where I can find a *"señorita,"* they look at me strangely and continue walking quickly. Out of curiosity, I keep moving with this flood of people flowing in one direction.

When I finally reach a knot of people a few blocks down the street, I find myself facing a human wall with hardly any space to go through. Male and female Indian voices scream out their lungs in Quechua. I have no idea what they are saying. Curiosity makes me eager to find out what is beyond that huge human forest. I move into it by pushing whoever is in front of me, drawing myself along by pulling their clothes down toward me as though ringing a church bell. I look up toward the sky, but can't see it. Instead, I see surprised faces looking down at me. I don't say a word but continue making my way forward.

Finally, the last obstacle in front of me is a woman, just standing there. She doesn't seem to notice I am holding her dress with my left hand and waving my right hand upward toward her head. It is as if her thick, circular dress isn't connected to her. I don't know what to do. The excited crowd is closing around me, tighter and tighter. And the legs of the people next to me push my small body toward the back of this woman, who then screams and cries out. Later on, I find out she is the wife of one of the two men in front of the crowd.

I decide to crawl under the woman. When I reach the other side of her and come out from between her legs, I encounter her face, so surprised that all she does is push me away. It must be a hard push because I end up sitting on the ground in the first row of onlookers. What I see in front of me is confusing, and I don't know what to make of it. There are two Indian men fighting like in the story of David and Goliath that my mother once told me. But neither of them seems a giant like Goliath. They are rather small men who furiously throw stones at each other, one at a time.

I look in the direction of the woman who placed me in first row. No one seems to exist around her. She only has eyes for one of the men. Suddenly, her mouth opens wide and the crooked gesture of her lips gives me a glimpse of her teeth. Her hands move fast toward her face as if they are trying to stop what is about to come out of her mouth. As her knees buckle to the ground, a loud crying sound comes out of her mouth, and the hands on her face seem unable to block the anguish from what she is witnessing. I turn my small head as fast as I can in the direction where her eyes are looking. I see one of the men falling down to the ground, while an explosion of blood comes out of his head. My eyes nearly escape from my face as they witness life and death dance together and death rise victorious. The body of the dead Indian man hitting the ground creates the sound of death that reverberates through the silence of the crowd.

**TINKU**

11

Then, the cry of the Indian woman rips that second of silence like a piece of paper being torn in two. Afterward, like the notes of a contrapuntal melody, a new sound comes into perspective: the sound of footsteps, some moving fast, some slow. They have as a background the crying sound of the woman, whose pain seems fused with the wind. Four Indian men arrive and lift the dead man from the ground on their shoulders to carry him away like a dead bird with broken wings. They pass nearby me. My eyes capture the blood still coming out of his head and hitting the dusty ground like drops of rain. I watch the men move toward the mountains in a procession of death. Behind them, his widow follows the path of an unknown future.

I still feel the wind on my face, and the woman's cries echo in my ears when, suddenly, I feel myself lifted and turned around to end up in my mother's arms. She and my father have been looking for me since they noticed my disappearance from my uncle's house. She asks with a trembling voice, "Are you all right?"

I look at her, then turn my head in the direction where the group of Indians are going. I say to her, "Yes. I was only looking for a *señorita*."

She hugs me hard. "I will get you one."

I know she will, because my mother understands I mean a carrot.

That night I eat a carrot dish with a sauce made of tomatoes and eggs. It is served with steamed chicken and potatoes. I learn from my uncle Zenón that what I witnessed that day was a *tinku*, Quechua for "encounter." This fight between two men from different Indian communities is still done once a year in the northern part of Potosi, enabling both communities to settle their differences. My uncle explains the Indian communities' belief that the death is good for the harvest that year. I don't understand this. As I taste the warmth of the carrot dish in my mouth, I think about the expression of pain on the Indian woman's face. At that moment, I sense that the image will stay with me for many years.

# *Quesillo* Cheese

The Bolivian cheese called *quesillo* comes from the state of Cochabamba. I find the flavor to be very close to feta cheese. *Quesillo* is used in the preparation of many recipes, including salads and empanadas, as well as being baked on top of a roll, known as tortilla. It is also eaten with corn, and in other dishes. *Quesillo* can be found easily in most Bolivian food markets. When accompanying many dishes such as *chicharrón de cerdo*, it is used fresh. However, it is also used dry in a variety of other dishes, or with toasted corn. Making your own *quesillo* is quite easy and fun. Rennet tablets are available in many supermarkets or at www.cheesesupply.com.

| ½ rennet tablet | 8 cups whole milk |
| --- | --- |
| 2¼ teaspoons salt | |

In a clay mortar with a wooden pestle, smash the rennet tablet. Add ¼ teaspoon of the salt and 2 teaspoons water. Mix well.

Heat the milk in a pot over low heat and very slowly, stirring, add the rennet mixture. Continue stirring for 2-3 minutes.

Pour the milk mixture into a bowl and set aside to curdle for 40-50 minutes. After the milk has cooled completely, slice it into 2-inch squares. Pour them into a strainer, cover with cheese cloth and leave them like this overnight in the refrigerator to get rid of the whey.

Add the remaining 2 teaspoons salt to the curds. With your hands mold the curds into 4 patties. Place them in the refrigerator for 5-6 hours and afterwards they'll be ready to eat.

# Locoto Sauce

*Uchu llajwa*, Quechua for "hot sauce," is made with a chili called *locoto*, similar to a small jalapeño. Another traditional ingredient is *quilquiña*, which I have replaced with cilantro. The result is not identical to the Bolivian *uchu llajwa*, but it is a good approximation. *Uchu llajwa* is used in soups, and on top of other dishes.

| | |
|---|---|
| 2 cups chopped tomato | 1 teaspoon minced fresh cilantro |
| 2 red or green jalapeños, seeded | ¼ teaspoon salt |
| ¼ cup chopped green bell peppers | 1½ teaspoons minced white onion |

In a mortar and pestle or food processor, puree all the ingredients except the onion.

**14** Just prior to serving, combine the mixture with the onion in a small bowl.

# Avocado Salad

Bolivians call avocado by the name *palta* and use it to accompany their meals in salads such as this one. Different types of avocados are grown in different parts of the country such as the Chapare area in the state of Cochabamba, as well as in the states bordering Brazil like Pando, Beni, and Santa Cruz.

| | |
|---|---|
| 6 large lettuce leaves | ½ teaspoon salt, or to taste |
| 3 avocados, peeled, pitted, and halved | ½ teaspoon ground black pepper |
| 1 cup peeled, minced tomato | 1 teaspoon white wine vinegar |
| ¼ cup minced white onion | 1 teaspoon olive oil |

Place a lettuce leaf on 6 salad plates. Set an avocado half on each leaf.

In a bowl, combine the tomato, onion, salt, pepper, vinegar, and oil. Spoon the mixture into each avocado half and serve.

**15**

**Note:** Make this salad just prior to serving, because avocado tends to brown quickly.

# Banana Squash *Lojro*

If you love the sweet flavor of banana squash, this is the perfect vegetable accompaniment.

| | |
|---|---|
| 4 large dried red chilies | 1 medium-size banana squash, peeled and cut into 1-inch cubes |
| 1 tablespoon olive oil | |
| 1 tablespoon minced garlic | 8 ears corn, shucked and cut into 2-inch pieces |
| 2 cups minced white onion | |
| 1 cup minced, peeled tomato | ½ cup fava beans, peeled |
| ½ teaspoon salt | ½ cup peas |
| ½ teaspoon ground black pepper | 3 medium-size potatoes, quartered |
| ½ teaspoon cumin | 16 slices *quesillo* or feta cheese |
| | 2 tablespoons minced fresh parsley |

**16**

Seed the dried chilies and soak in warm water until soft. Drain and squeeze dry. In a mortar and pestle or food processor, process the chilies until they form a smooth paste.

In a pot over medium heat, heat the oil and fry the garlic and onion until light brown and crisp. Add the tomato, salt, pepper, cumin, and chili paste, and cook for 10 minutes.

Add the squash, corn, and water to cover, and cook for 5 minutes. Add the fava beans, peas, and potatoes and cook for 25 minutes, until potatoes are tender.

Drain the liquid and transfer to a serving platter. Top with the parsley and cheese. Serve hot.

# Banana Squash Fritters

*Bocadillos de Calabaza*                    6 servings

The sweet taste of banana squash makes this recipe a great snack for anytime.

| | |
|---|---|
| 2 cups diced, steamed banana squash | ¼ teaspoon salt |
| 2 eggs, lightly beaten | ¼ cup olive oil |
| ¼ teaspoon ground black pepper | |

In a bowl, combine the banana squash, eggs, pepper, and salt. Form the mixture into ½-inch-thick, 3-inch-diameter patties.

Heat the oil in a flat-bottom pan over medium heat, and fry the patties until golden brown on both sides.

17

# Beet Salad

Beets are known in Bolivia and Chile as *betarragas*. In other Latin American countries they are called *remolachas*.

| | |
|---|---|
| 4½ pounds beets | 1 teaspoon white wine vinegar |
| ½ teaspoon salt | 1 teaspoon olive oil |
| ½ teaspoon ground black pepper | |

Peel and boil the beets until they are soft and tender. Shred into fine strands with a knife, to make 6 cups.

In a bowl, combine the beets, salt, pepper, vinegar, and oil.

Serve with any type of roast.

18

# Cauliflower Salad

This nutritious vegetable is quite tasty served in a salad. Cauliflower is used often during the summer when it is in season, especially in the valley regions. It is also used in soups.

| | |
|---|---|
| 2 medium-size heads cauliflower | 2 teaspoons white wine vinegar |
| 1 teaspoon salt | 1 tablespoon olive oil |
| ½ teaspoon ground black pepper | |

Bring salted water to a boil in a pot over medium heat, and cook the cauliflower until soft. Drain and rinse with cold water.

Cut the cauliflower into 1-inch pieces.

In a bowl, combine the cauliflower, salt, pepper, vinegar, and oil.

Serve with any type of roast.

19

# Mashed Cauliflower

Mashed cauliflower is a great replacement for mashed potatoes and ideal for people concerned about eating too many carbohydrates.

| | |
|---|---|
| 2 large heads cauliflower | ¼ teaspoon salt |
| 5 tablespoons butter | ¼ teaspoon ground black pepper |
| ½ cup evaporated milk | |

Trim and discard the green stalks from the cauliflower. Cut the cauliflower into small pieces.

Put the cauliflower in a large pot with water to cover and bring to a boil. Cook until tender, 15–20 minutes. Mash the cauliflower with the butter, evaporated milk, salt, and pepper.

# Cooked Cabbage Salad

This soft, tasty salad goes well with boiled corn and baked or fried chicken.

| | |
|---|---|
| 2 medium-size heads cabbage, shredded | 1 teaspoon white wine vinegar |
| ½ teaspoon salt, or to taste | 1 tablespoon olive oil |
| ½ teaspoon ground pepper | |

Bring 8 cups of water to a boil, and add the cabbage. Cook until the cabbage is soft. Remove, drain, and chop.

In a bowl, combine the cabbage with the rest of the ingredients. Toss to mix well.

Serve cold.

21

# Raw Cabbage Salad

The crunchy texture of this salad makes it a good complement to the various meat dishes in this book.

| | |
|---|---|
| 6 cups minced cabbage | 1 teaspoon white wine vinegar |
| ½ teaspoon salt | 1 tablespoon olive oil |
| ½ teaspoon ground black pepper | |

Place the cabbage in a bowl, add hot water to cover it and soak 5 minutes. Drain, and repeat this procedure three times. Then, cover the cabbage with cold water and let soak 5 minutes. Drain.

Combine the cabbage with the rest of the ingredients. Toss to mix well.

**22**

# Boiled Dry Corn

*Mote de maíz* is a popular dish eaten with *quesillo* cheese. When I was growing up in Bolivia, this dish was traditionally eaten at a bonfire celebrating Saint John's Eve on June 23. This dish is also a good snack. The type of corn usually used for this dish is called *willkaparu*, the Quechua word for zea corn, which is a dark corn. *Mote* can also be made from yellow or white corn.

| |
|---|
| 2 cups dry white corn or hominy |

Rinse the corn well and soak in 8 cups of water overnight.

Strain the corn into a pot, and bring the soaking liquid to a boil. Add the corn, reduce the heat, and simmer for 3–4 hours, until the corn kernels bursts.

**23**

# Cucumber Salad
# with Quesillo

*Ensalada de Pepinos con Quesillo*                    **6 servings**

This salad is served with a variety of dishes, such as *chicharrón de cerdo* (page 133) and *charque* (page 111).

| | |
|---|---|
| 4 cups peeled, diced cucumber | 1 teaspoon minced fresh cilantro |
| 2 cups crumbled *quesillo* or feta cheese | 1 teaspoon white wine vinegar |
| | 1 tablespoon olive oil |
| 1 cup peeled, minced tomato | 6 unpeeled red potatoes, boiled |

In a bowl, combine the cucumber with the rest of the ingredients. Toss to mix well.

24

# Fava Beans

This *mote* tastes great prepared with peeled or unpeeled fava beans. In Bolivia, *motes* are accompanied by other dishes or served as a snack.

| 4 cups fava beans, peeled | 1 teaspoon salt |
|---|---|

Steam the fava beans over salted water for 10–15 minutes, until they are soft and wrinkled.

Serve hot with a piece of *quesillo* or feta cheese.

**25**

# Favas *Pejtu*

*Pejtu* is a Quechua word meaning mixture. The combination of dried beef and fava beans is usually prepared during the summertime when fava beans are abundant in the valley regions of Bolivia.

| | |
|---|---|
| 4 large dried red chilies | 1 tablespoon seedless, ground red chili |
| 2 tablespoons olive oil | |
| 2 cups minced white onion | ½ cup minced tomato |
| 1 teaspoon minced garlic | ¼ cup minced fresh parsley |
| ½ teaspoon cumin | 2 cups beef broth |
| 1 teaspoon dried oregano | 5 cups fava beans, peeled |
| ½ teaspoon ground black pepper | ¼ pound *charque* (page 111) |
| ½ teaspoon salt | 6 potatoes, peeled and boiled |

**26**

Seed the chilies and soak in warm water until soft. Drain and squeeze dry. In a mortar and pestle or food processor, process the chilies until they form a smooth paste.

Heat the oil in a saucepan over medium heat, and sauté the onion and garlic until light brown and crisp. Add the cumin, oregano, pepper, salt, and chili paste. Cook for 5 minutes. Add the tomato, parsley, and broth. Cook for 25 minutes.

Bring 6 cups of water to a boil in a pot over medium heat, and add the fava beans a few at a time without letting the boiling stop. Add the *charque* and cook for 5 minutes. Remove the meat and set it aside. Cook the favas for 20 minutes longer, until they are soft. Remove from the heat and drain.

Cut the dried beef into 2-inch pieces. Add the favas and dried beef to the onion mixture and cook for 10 minutes.

Serve with the potatoes.

# Radish Salad

This tangy salad is eaten with meat dishes like *charque* (page 111) or *enrollado* (page 136).

| | |
|---|---|
| 4 cups minced radish | 1 teaspoon white wine vinegar |
| ½ teaspoon salt | 1 tablespoon olive oil |

In a bowl, combine all of the ingredients and toss to mix well.

**Variation:** Add 1 cup crumbled *quesillo* or feta cheese.

27

# Spinach and Swiss Chard Stew

**4 servings**

The unique combination of turkey, spinach, and Swiss chard makes for a tasty meal.

| | |
|---|---|
| 2 cups chopped Swiss chard | ½ cup minced tomato |
| 2 cups chopped spinach | ½ pound ground turkey |
| 1 tablespoon olive oil | ½ teaspoon ground black pepper |
| 1 cup minced white onion | ½ teaspoon salt |
| 1 teaspoon minced garlic | 4 large potatoes, peeled and boiled |

Steam the Swiss chard and spinach for 5–7 minutes, until soft. Do not overcook. Remove from the heat and let cool.

**28**

Heat the oil in a saucepan over medium heat, and sauté the onion and garlic until light brown and crisp. Add the tomato, turkey, pepper, salt, Swiss chard, and spinach. Reduce the heat to a simmer and cook until the meat is cooked through.

Serve with the boiled potatoes.

# *Cochabambino* Salad

The peculiar moniker of this salad refers to the valley region of the state of Cochabamba. *Soltero* means "single" and implies that the salad is easy to make.

| | |
|---|---|
| 2 cups crumbled *quesillo* or feta cheese | 1 tablespoon minced fresh parsley |
| 1 cup minced tomato | 1 tablespoon minced fresh cilantro |
| 2 tablespoons minced bell pepper | ½ teaspoon ground black pepper |
| | 1½ cups finely sliced white onion |

In a bowl, combine all the ingredients, adding the onion last.

Serve with any type of roast.

29

# Lettuce Salad

*Ensalada de Lechuga*                                                    6 servings

Crunchy fresh lettuce is the main ingredient in this salad, which is simple to make and part of many Bolivian meals.

| | |
|---|---|
| 2 heads iceberg lettuce, chopped | ½ teaspoon ground black pepper |
| 1 white onion, thinly sliced | 1 teaspoon white wine vinegar |
| 1 cup minced tomato | 1 tablespoon olive oil |
| ½ teaspoon salt | |

Combine all the ingredients in a bowl. Toss well and serve immediately to preserve the freshness of the lettuce.

30

# Mixed Salad

This is a good salad to accompany any meat, and its ingredients are easily found in most markets in the U.S.

| | |
|---|---|
| ½ cup peeled and diced carrots, cooked | ½ teaspoon salt |
| 1 cup fava beans, peeled and cooked | ½ teaspoon ground black pepper |
| ½ cup green peas, cooked | 1 teaspoon white wine vinegar |
| 1 cup peeled, diced potatoes, cooked | 1 tablespoon olive oil |
| ½ cup diced white onion | 6 lettuce leaves |
| 1 cup peeled, diced tomato | |

In a bowl, combine all the ingredients except the lettuce, mixing well.

Serve the mixture on top of the lettuce leaves.

31

# Raw Salsa

*Salsa cruda* is used in salads and on warm dishes, such as *sill'panchu* (page 127) and *chuño phuti* (page 34). This recipe lacks one traditional ingredient, *quillquiña*, an aromatic herb with small, dark green leaves, traditionally used in salsas. *Quillquiña* is not available in the U.S., but I have replaced it with cilantro.

| | |
|---|---|
| ½ cup minced white onion | 1 tablespoon minced fresh cilantro |
| ½ cup minced, peeled tomato | ¼ teaspoon salt |
| 1 tablespoon minced bell pepper | |

In a bowl, combine all the ingredients. Make this salad just prior to serving.

32

# Freeze-Dried Potatoes

*Chuño* is the Quechua word for freeze-dried potatoes. Centuries ago, the Incas dried potatoes in order to preserve them. *Chuño* was made during the winter because four consecutive cold nights were required. Then, the potatoes were pressed to extract the water and dried in the sun. The result was a shrunken, freeze-dried potato, which kept for years.
In most Bolivian markets these days, it is possible to buy freeze-dried potatoes of various colors and sizes. When I visit my sisters in Bolivia, I bring a supply of such potatoes home to the U.S. However, my mother taught me how to freeze potatoes in the freezer and thus to create my own *chuño* away from Bolivia. This technique works very well. Freezing the potatoes gives them a nutty taste and texture and, most importantly, it is very easy to make.

---

12 small potatoes

**33**

Rinse the potatoes in cold water and dry them thoroughly before placing them in the freezer overnight. They can be kept frozen for a couple months.

Soak the freeze-dried potatoes overnight in plenty of warm water. Peel the potatoes and break them into small pieces with your hands. Rinse the *chuño* 5 or 6 times, squeezing out the water with your hands to eliminate the sour taste.

The potatoes are ready to be made into *chuño phuti* (page 34).

**CONDIMENTS, SALADS, AND SIDE DISHES**

# Sautéed Freeze-Dried Potatoes

This side dish is frequently served with *picante de pollo* (page 99) and spicy tongue (page 148). Because potatoes are available in many colors in Bolivia, *chuño phuti* can be dark or white. Regardless of the color, both of them taste very much the same. Although *chuño* is different from regular potatoes, its nutty flavor will win you over.

| | |
|---|---|
| 2 cups *chuño* (page 33) | **Salsa:** |
| 2 teaspoons salt | 1 tablespoon olive oil |
| 2 tablespoons olive oil | ½ cup minced white onion |
| ½ cup minced white onion | ½ cup minced, peeled tomato |
| ¼ cup minced, peeled tomato | 1 teaspoon minced fresh parsley |
| 3 eggs | ½ teaspoon salt |
| 1 cup crumbled *quesillo* or feta cheese | ½ teaspoon ground black pepper |

34

Bring 10 cups water to a boil in a large pot and add the *chuño* and salt. Change the water as soon as it starts boiling. Cook until the *chuño* is tender and slightly crunchy. Drain and set aside.

Heat the oil in a saucepan over medium heat, and fry the onion until light brown and crisp. Add the tomato and cook for 5 minutes. Add the eggs and stir well.

In a pot, combine the onion mixture with the drained *chuño*. Stir and simmer for about 5 minutes. A few minutes prior to serving, add the cheese and stir.

**For the salsa:** Mix all the ingredients together in a bowl and pour over the *chuño phuti*. Serve hot.

# Huancaina-Style Potatoes

Yellow chilies make this a particularly attractive dish, with hard-boiled eggs and potatoes peeking through the sauce.

| | |
|---|---|
| 4 whole dried yellow chilies | 8 lettuce leaves |
| 2 tablespoons olive oil | 4 medium-size potatoes, peeled and |
| ½ teaspoon salt | boiled |
| ½ teaspoon ground black pepper | 1 hard-boiled egg |
| 1 cup ground roasted peanuts | 8 black olives, pitted |
| 1 cup crumbled *quesillo* or feta cheese | |

Seed the chilies and soak in warm water until soft. Drain and squeeze dry. In a mortar and pestle or food processor, process the chilies until they form a smooth paste.

In a saucepan over medium heat, heat the oil and sauté the chili paste for 2 minutes. Add the salt, pepper, peanuts, and ¼ cup water. Cook for 5 minutes.

Add the cheese and stir until melted. Remove from the heat and set aside.

Arrange the lettuce leaves on a platter and pile the hot potatoes on top. Pour the chili sauce over the potatoes. Garnish with slices of egg and the olives. Serve hot.

**35**

# Potatoes with Ham and Onions

In this recipe potatoes combine perfectly with ham to make a great snack.

| | |
|---|---|
| 2 tablespoons olive oil | 1 cup chopped ham |
| 1 cup minced white onion | 2 bay leaves |
| 10 small potatoes, peeled and halved | 2 whole cloves |

In a pot over medium heat, heat the oil. Add the remaining ingredients and cook at a simmer, uncovered, until the potatoes are soft. Add 1 cup water and cook for 15 minutes longer.

36

# Potato Casserole

There are many variations of dishes that include potatoes. This casserole works wonderfully for dinner.

| | |
|---|---|
| 6 large potatoes, peeled | ¼ cup peeled minced tomato |
| 2 teaspoons salt | 1 cup finely chopped sirloin steak |
| ¼ cup butter | ¼ cup minced fresh parsley |
| 3 egg yolks, lightly beaten | ½ cup beef broth |
| 1 teaspoon sugar | ½ teaspoon salt |
| ½ teaspoon ground black pepper | ½ teaspoon ground black pepper |
| | ¼ cup raisins |
| **Filling:** | 8 green olives, pitted |
| 2 teaspoons olive oil | 1 hard-boiled egg, sliced |
| ½ cup minced white onion | 1 egg white, lightly beaten |

37

Preheat the oven to 350°F. Grease an 8-inch pan.

Boil the potatoes with the salt in a pot over medium heat until they can be mashed easily. Remove from the heat and drain.

Mash with the butter, egg yolks, sugar, and pepper.

**For the filling:** Heat the oil in a saucepan over medium heat, and sauté the onion until light brown and crisp. Add the tomato, steak, parsley, broth, salt, and pepper. Reduce the heat to a simmer and cook until the meat is cooked through.

Spread half of the mashed potatoes in the prepared pan and spread the meat mixture evenly on top. Evenly distribute the olives and egg slices, and pour the other half of the potatoes on top. Brush the top of the mashed potatoes with the egg white and bake for 15–20 minutes. Serve hot.

# Stuffed Potato Balls

These potato balls can be stuffed with a filling of meat, cheese, or chicken. Served with a lettuce salad, it makes a good meal.

| For the Potatoes: | 2 tablespoons butter |
|---|---|
| 6 large baking potatoes, peeled | ½ cup plus 1 tablespoon evaporated milk |
| ½ teaspoon salt, or to taste | 3 eggs, lightly beaten |
| ½ teaspoon ground black pepper | 3 tablespoons flour |

Bring 8 cups water to a boil in a pot, and add the potatoes, ¼ teaspoon of the salt, and the pepper. The water should cover the potatoes by about 1 inch. Cook until the potatoes are tender. Drain.

**38**

Mash the potatoes while they are still hot. Add the butter, ½ cup of the evaporated milk, and the remaining ¼ teaspoon salt.

Preheat the oven to 350°F. Grease a baking sheet.

Form the mashed potatoes into medium-size potato shapes, enclosing about 1 teaspoon of filling in the middle.

In a bowl, combine the eggs, flour, and the remaining 1 tablespoon of evaporated milk. Brush the mixture on each potato.

Place the potatoes on the prepared baking sheet and bake for 10–15 minutes, or until golden brown. Remove from the oven and serve hot.

**Meat Filling:**

1 teaspoon olive oil

½ pound ground sirloin

1 teaspoon minced garlic

1 (15-ounce) can tomato sauce

½ cup red wine

1 tablespoon sugar

1 teaspoon grated orange zest

½ teaspoon salt, or to taste

**Cheese Filling:**

2 cups crumbled quesillo or feta
   cheese

**Chicken Filling:**

1 tablespoon olive oil

¼ cup minced white onion

1 teaspoon minced garlic

1 cup minced tomato

3 whole boneless, skinless chicken
   breasts, diced

¼ cup minced fresh parsley

½ teaspoon salt, or to taste

½ teaspoon ground black pepper

**For the meat filling:** Heat the oil in a saucepan over medium heat, and sauté the meat and garlic for 15 minutes. Add the tomato sauce and cook for 10 minutes. Reduce the heat to a simmer and add the wine, sugar, and orange zest. Cook until the juices dry up. Remove from the heat and set aside.

**For the chicken filling:** In a saucepan over medium heat, heat the oil and fry the onion and garlic until light brown and crispy. Add the tomato, chicken, parsley, salt, and pepper. Reduce the heat to simmer and cook until the chicken is cooked through.

# Steamed *Humintas*

These corn dumplings require a large-grained corn, which is hard to find in most U.S. supermarkets. I found a similar type in Mexico. It does not have the same texture as Bolivian corn, but it was a good substitute. The sweet corn available in the U.S. does not work, but you may find white corn with big kernels in some farmers' markets or Latin markets.

| | |
|---|---|
| 8 ears large-kerneled fresh corn, kernels removed and ground (4 cups), cobs and husks reserved | 1 cup crumbled plus 8 slices quesillo or feta cheese |
| 1 cup olive oil | 1 teaspoon aniseed |
| 1 teaspoon salt | 1 teaspoon ground cinnamon |
| 2 teaspoons sugar | Boiling water |
| | 1 small potato |

**40** In a bowl, mix the corn, oil, salt, sugar, 1 cup of the feta cheese, aniseed, and cinnamon.

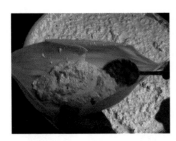

Place two corn husks side by side, slightly overlapping. Add ½ cup of the corn mixture and a slice of cheese. Fold up the bottom of the corn husk, then fold down the top, and lastly fold in both sides. Tie each *huminta* with a string made of corn husks (use the fiber from the edges of the extra husks to make the thread) with the knot on the folded side.

Place two layers of corn cobs in a pot, plus some extra corn husks. Pour boiling water to cover the first layer of the corn cobs. Add the *humintas* and cover them with more corn husks. Simmer for 45 minutes, along with a small potato. When the potato is cooked, so are the *humintas*.

# Baked *Humintas*

When I visit my family in Bolivia, I return with a suitcase full of frozen *humintas* in order to enjoy their flavor for many more days. This type of *huminta* is different from the steamed ones, because it is baked and has a firmer consistency.

| | |
|---|---|
| 8 ears corn, ground (4 cups) | 1 teaspoon aniseed |
| 1 cup olive oil | 1 teaspoon ground cinnamon |
| 1 teaspoon salt | 8 fresh corn husks |
| 2 teaspoons sugar | |

Preheat the oven to 350°F.

In a bowl, mix the corn, oil, salt, sugar, aniseed, and cinnamon.

41

Spread ½ cup of the corn mixture on the lower half of each corn husk. Fold down the top, then fold in the sides.

Place the *humintas*, folded edges down, on a baking sheet and bake for 30 minutes.

Serve hot with cinnamon tea or hot chocolate.

# Bolivian Tacos

**Tacos Bolivianos** **4 servings**

The first time I made tacos was in the '70s, when I went from Mexico back to Bolivia for a visit. My family's reaction to Mexican tortillas was the same as mine the first time I ate them, which was not positive. My sister Mary and my niece Gina thought they tasted like raw dough. These days, however, tacos are one of the most popular foods among my family in Bolivia. The following recipe does not use refried beans, to keep the carbohydrates down for people concerned about their weight. Low-carbohydrate tortillas can be found in such stores as Trader Joe's.

| | |
|---|---|
| 3 tablespoons olive oil | 1 teaspoon grated orange zest |
| 1 cup minced white onion | 1 avocado |
| 1 tablespoon minced garlic | 1 cup minced tomato |
| 6 ounces white mushrooms, sliced | 1 teaspoon minced fresh cilantro |
| 1 pound lean ground sirloin | 16 ounces mozzarella cheese, cut into ¼-inch slices |
| ¼ teaspoon salt | |
| 1 (15-ounce) can tomato sauce | 2 cups chopped lettuce |
| ½ cup red wine | 8 whole-wheat tortillas |
| 1½ teaspoons sugar | |

Heat 2 tablespoons of the oil in a saucepan over medium heat, and sauté the onion and garlic until light brown and crisp. Add the mushrooms and cook for 5 minutes. Add the meat and ⅛ teaspoon of the salt, and cook for 20 minutes until the onion breaks down. Add the tomato sauce and cook for 10 more minutes. Reduce the heat to a simmer and add the wine, sugar, and orange zest. Cook until the juices evaporate. Keep warm at a low simmer.

Preheat the broiler.

In a bowl, mash the avocado with a fork. Add the tomato, cilantro, remaining 1 tablespoon oil, and remaining ⅛ teaspoon salt. Set aside.

Layer the cheese in an 8-inch ceramic casserole dish. Broil the cheese for 5–7 minutes until completely melted and golden brown on top.

In a pan over medium heat warm the tortillas one by one. Layer the meat, cheese, lettuce, and guacamole on the tortillas.

**MY MOTHER'S BOLIVIAN KITCHEN**

# Cheese Omelet

The cheesy taste of this omelet is a good addition to the tea and bread served for breakfast.

| | |
|---|---|
| 1 tablespoon olive oil | ½ cup crumbled *quesillo* or feta or cheddar cheese |
| 2 eggs, lightly beaten | |

Heat the oil in a small skillet over medium heat, then add the eggs and cheese, stirring well. Cook the tortilla, flipping halfway, until lightly browned on both sides.

43

# Baked Macaroni Casserole

In Bolivian cuisine, pasta is often used in soups and casseroles. The cheese in this dish makes it very appealing for those who love the flavor of *quesillo* or feta.

| | |
|---|---|
| 1 pound macaroni | ½ cup beef broth |
| 2½ teaspoons salt | 3 eggs, lightly beaten |
| 2 tablespoons olive oil | ½ cup milk |
| 1 cup minced white onion | 2 hard-boiled eggs, sliced |
| ½ cup minced, peeled tomato | 12 ounces *quesillo* or feta cheese, cut in ¼-inch slices |
| 1 teaspoon minced fresh parsley | |
| ½ teaspoon ground black pepper | 2 tablespoons butter, melted |

**44**

Cook the macaroni in boiling water with 1 teaspoon of the salt until al dente, about 15 minutes. Drain and set aside.

Preheat the oven to 350°F. Grease an 8-inch pan.

In a pot over medium heat, heat 1 tablespoon of the olive oil and sauté the onion until light brown and crisp. Add the tomato, parsley, pepper, broth, and 1 teaspoon of salt. Cook for 15 minutes, then remove from the heat.

Combine the eggs, milk and remaining ½ teaspoon salt in a bowl. Add the macaroni and mix well.

Pour half of the macaroni mixture into the prepared pan. Spread the tomato sauce on top of the macaroni, and top with half of the sliced hard-boiled eggs and the cheese. Add the rest of the macaroni mixture and then the remaining sliced eggs and cheese on top. Pour the melted butter over the *pastel* and bake for 20 minutes.

Serve hot.

# Baked Rice Casserole

This side dish can be served with any kind of meat.

| | |
|---|---|
| 2 cups white rice | ½ cup beef broth |
| ½ teaspoon dried oregano | ½ teaspoon salt, or to taste |
| 2 eggs, lightly beaten | ½ teaspoon ground black pepper |
| 1 tablespoon olive oil | 8 slices *quesillo* or feta cheese |
| ½ cup minced white onion | 2 hard-boiled eggs, sliced into eighths |
| ½ cup minced, peeled tomato | 6 black olives, pitted and halved |
| ¼ cup minced fresh parsley | |

In a pot over medium heat, bring 4 cups water to a boil, then add the rice. Return to a boil, then reduce the heat to a simmer and cook until tender, 15 minutes. Remove from the heat and set aside.

Preheat the oven to 350°F. Grease an 8-inch pan.

Heat the oil in a saucepan over medium heat, and sauté the onion until light brown and crisp. Add the tomato, parsley, broth, salt, and pepper. Cook for 15 minutes and remove from the heat.

In a bowl, mix the eggs with the cooked rice.

Pour half of the rice mixture into the prepared pan. Top with half the sauce and then half of the hard-boiled eggs, olives, and cheese. Layer the remaining rice mixture, then the sauce, eggs, and cheese in the pan. Pour the melted butter over the *pastel* and bake for 15 minutes.

Serve hot.

45

# Rice with *Quesillo*

This cheese and rice dish is a good complement to any meat.

| | |
|---|---|
| 1 cup white rice | ¼ cup evaporated milk |
| ½ cup crumbled *quesillo* or feta cheese | |

Bring 2 cups water to a boil in a pot, and add the rice, stirring constantly. Add the cheese and evaporated milk. Reduce the heat and simmer for 15–20 minutes, until the rice is tender.

Serve with roast beef or any other meat.

46

# Toasted Rice

*Arroz Graneado*                                                      **4 servings**

Preparing rice this way prevents it from becoming sticky. It is customary in Bolivia to prepare this dish to accompany meat or poultry.

| | |
|---|---|
| 1 tablespoon olive oil | ½ teaspoon salt |
| 1 cup rice | ⅛ teaspoon ground black pepper |

Heat the oil in a saucepan over medium heat, and sauté the rice until light brown. Remove from the heat and set aside.

In a pot, bring 2 cups water to a boil and add the rice, salt, and pepper. Reduce the heat and simmer for 15–20 minutes until the rice is cooked.

47

# Quinoa Fritters

Besides being nutritious, these snacks can be made a day ahead and fried when you need them.

| | |
|---|---|
| 1 cup quinoa | 1 teaspoon minced garlic |
| ½ teaspoon salt | ½ cup peeled, minced tomato |
| ½ cup crumbled *quesillo* or feta cheese | ½ cup minced fresh parsley |
| 2 eggs, lightly beaten | ½ teaspoon cumin |
| ¼ cup plus 1 tablespoon olive oil | ¼ teaspoon ground black pepper |
| 1 cup minced white onion | 2 cups chicken broth |

Bring 3 cups water to a boil, add the quinoa, and cook for 15 minutes. Reduce the heat to a simmer and cook for 50 more minutes, until the water has almost completely evaporated. Remove from the heat.

Add ¼ teaspoon of the salt, the cheese, and eggs to the quinoa. Stir well. Form the mixture into ½-inch thick, 3-inch-diameter patties.

In a saucepan over medium heat, heat 1 tablespoon of the oil and fry the onion and garlic until light brown and crisp. Add the tomato, parsley, cumin, pepper, broth, and remaining ¼ teaspoon of the salt, and cook for 35 minutes, until the onion breaks down.

Heat the remaining ¼ cup of oil in a flat-bottom pan over medium heat, and fry the patties until golden brown on both sides. Remove from heat.

Top each fritter with a tablespoon of the onion mixture and serve.

**48**

# Quinoa Stew

**P'isque de Quinua**

For thousands of years, quinoa has been cultivated in the Altiplano regions of Bolivia. It continues to be part of Bolivian cuisine and is used in a variety of recipes. The Quechua word *p'isque* means "stew."

| | |
|---|---|
| ½ cup quinoa | ½ cup chicken broth |
| 1 tablespoon olive oil | ½ cup milk |
| ½ cup minced white onion | ½ cup *quesillo* or feta cheese |
| ½ cup peeled, minced tomato | 2 eggs |
| 2 tablespoons minced fresh parsley | 4 potatoes, peeled and boiled |

In a pot over medium heat, combine 1½ cups water and the quinoa. Bring to a boil, then reduce the heat to a simmer. Continue cooking until the quinoa pops and all the liquid is absorbed, 45–55 minutes. Set aside.

Heat the oil in a pan over medium heat, and sauté the onion until crisp. Add the tomato, parsley, and chicken broth, and cook for 15 minutes. Reduce the heat to a simmer and add the quinoa, and then the milk to the onion mixture.

Stir in the cheese. When the mixture boils, add the eggs. Stir until the eggs are cooked.

Serve hot with the potatoes.

# Boiled Yucca

Boiled yucca is eaten mostly in the regions of the Amazon such as Pando, Beni and Santa Cruz, but it is also found on the tables of other states in the valley region. It is served similar to potatoes to accompany meat dishes.

| | |
|---|---|
| 2 medium-size yuccas | ½ teaspoon ground black pepper |
| ½ teaspoon salt | |

Peel the yuccas and slice into 3-inch pieces. Halve, and remove the core.

Bring 8 cups water to a boil in a pot, and add the yucca, salt, and pepper. Cook for 20 minutes, until almost tender. Drain and set aside. Do not overcook or the pieces will become mushy and fall apart.

**50**

Serve hot with *chicharrón* (page 133) or any other meat dish.

# Fried Yucca

Fried yucca tastes similar to a fried potato, but more breadlike. In the Amazon regions of Bolivia, yucca is preferred over potatoes and is eaten as part of daily meals.

| | |
|---|---|
| 2 medium-size yuccas | ½ teaspoon ground black pepper |
| ½ teaspoon salt | 2 tablespoons olive oil |

Peel the yuccas and slice into 3-inch pieces. Halve, and remove the fibrous core.

Bring 8 cups water to a boil in a pot, and add the yucca, salt, and pepper. Cook for 20 minutes, until almost tender. Drain and set aside. Do not overcook or the pieces will become mushy and fall apart.

In a pan over medium heat, heat the oil and fry the yucca until light brown. Drain on paper towels.

51

# Fried Stuffed Yucca

Yucca (cassava or manioc root) is usually eaten in the states of Beni, Santa Cruz, and Pando, which border Brazil. Variations of this dish are found in other states like Cochabamba, where my sister Guichy makes it for me when I visit her. Yucca is also eaten quite a lot in the Caribbean. It can be purchased at many supermarkets in the U.S. I have found that this dish is quite popular among my friends here.

| Yucca: | ½ teaspoon ground black pepper |
| --- | --- |
| 2 large yuccas | 2 tablespoons olive oil |
| ½ teaspoon salt | |

Peel the yucca and slice into 3-inch pieces. Halve, and remove the core.

Bring 8 cups water to a boil in a pot, and add the yucca, salt, and pepper. The water should cover the yucca by 1 inch. Cook for 20 minutes, until almost tender. Drain and set aside. Do not overcook or the pieces will become mushy and fall apart.

In a bowl, mash the yucca while it is still hot, as if making mashed potatoes.

**To make the patties:** Form the mashed yucca into 1-inch thick, 3-inch-diameter patties enclosing about 1 teaspoon of cheese, chicken, or meat filling in the middle. In a flat-bottomed pan over medium heat, heat the oil and fry the patties until golden brown on both sides.

52

| Meat Filling: | Cheese Filling: |
|---|---|
| 1 teaspoon olive oil | 2 cups crumbled *quesillo* or feta cheese |
| ½ pound ground sirloin | |
| 1 teaspoon minced garlic | |
| 1 (15-ounce) can tomato sauce | Chicken Filling: |
| ½ cup red wine | 3 whole boneless, skinless chicken breasts |
| 1 tablespoon sugar | |
| 1 teaspoon grated orange zest | ½ teaspoon salt |

**For the meat filling:** Heat the oil in a saucepan over medium heat, and sauté the meat and garlic for 15 minutes. Add the tomato sauce and cook for 10 minutes. Reduce the heat to a simmer and add the wine, sugar, and orange zest. Cook until the juices evaporate. Remove from the heat and set aside.

**53**

**For the chicken filling:** Bring 8 cups water to a boil in a pot, and add the chicken and salt. Cook for 45 minutes, until the chicken is tender. Remove from the heat and set aside to cool.

Finely shred the chicken and set aside.

# Yucca Salad

This is a version of a salad from the Amazon region of Bolivia that my wife Tina enjoys preparing for a cold summer lunch.

| | |
|---|---|
| 2 medium-size yuccas | 2 tablespoons olive oil |
| ½ teaspoon ground black pepper | 1 cup Spanish green olives |
| 1 tablespoon white wine vinegar | |

Peel the yuccas and slice into 1-inch pieces. Halve and remove the core.

Bring 8 cups water to a boil in a pot, and add the yucca. Cook for 20 minutes until almost tender. Drain and set aside. Do not overcook or the pieces will become mushy and fall apart.

**54** In a bowl, combine the yucca, pepper, vinegar, oil, and olives. Chill the mixture in the refrigerator and serve cold.

# THE UNAVOIDABLE VISITOR

I have been present many times when death arrived as a visitor during her tiring work schedule, and the impression of seeing her has never diminished. My aunt Lina used to say that the first experience of witnessing this visit is hard to forget. Death is so generous with her time that she does not leave anyone out. It does not matter where you are or who are with, even if you are hiding reincarnated in a chosen animal.

The second time I saw the unavoidable visitor, she had placed two little stones on her eyes and wore a cotton summer dress that reached her knees. She was not wearing shoes. Her long brown hair looked as if it were part of the brown table where she lay. Her two small hands holding each other, never be separated again, looked like two birds making love. Her seven-year-old body lay there, cold and lifeless. Her name was Marta, or should I say that death took that name after she invaded the child's fragile body. Since then, I have seen this visitor many more times, but each time she uses a different name. It would seem that she is trying not to be noticed, and I would bet she travels incognito. This way, she can be any-where with anybody without even having to pay for her travels.

My aunt Maria had a special relationship with death throughout her life. Once, while I was visiting her house, one of her *comadres* came to see her early one evening and spoke in a broken voice, "Doña Maria, please could you let me know if my son is going to get well?" The *comadre's* name was Inés; that morning, she stood helplessly with her two-year-old son in her arms, insisting, "Doña Maria you know these things, please ..."

My aunt, as calm and peaceful as a yogi, slowly moved her skinny frame. She rubbed the child's entire body with *millu* (aluminum sulfate) and in a calm tone of voice murmured, "Let's burn the coal."

With the slowness of a cat that has just woken up from a nap, Aunt Maria walked toward the patio of her house and lit a fire, using some coal on the ground next to a small garden of flowers. The serenity of her expression did not seem to be perturbed by anything around her. I walked close to her, and then Inés approached us. I stood by the wooden chair that my aunt sat in. She blew on the coal, which held a flicker of fire. The flame gave in to my aunt's gust of air and very soon illuminated her face with its reddish yellow flames, which burned the *millu* my aunt threw into the flame.

Inés watched intensely as my aunt's head moved from side to side like the pendulum of an old clock ready to chime. The silence during that early evening at my aunt's house allowed any sound to be heard while Inés and I waited for her to speak. I heard the fire crackling and the melting noise made by the *millu* in the fire. I noticed that the intensity of the heat created shapes in the *millu* as it melted. Suddenly my aunt spoke in a sad and concerned voice, "Your child won't make it to tomorrow, poor little angel." Her eyes did not move from the fire as she kept watching the shapes formed by the millu. Then she added, pointing to the fire, "This is a grave ... no! Poor little angel he won't live ..." And the next morning, Inés' son had death inside him.

When I was seven years old I believed that Aunt Maria worked for death and that her job was to announce the arrival of the uninvited visitor in the body of people like Inés' son. I also thought that Aunt Maria did not agree with the modus operandi of her boss and that she had been hired without a choice.

That day, when I witnessed another of my aunt Maria's many death predictions, I was there because I was not feeling well. My body ached because I was getting a cold or something. In addition to the gift of predicting death, Aunt Maria also had the gift of healing. She had the most incredible hands, which could heal any pain, even a simple aching flu.

That afternoon before Inés arrived, I sat next to her and she touched behind my ears with her soft, soothing hands, saying, "Someone has scared you; you have a little bump here." While her fingers pressed behind my ears, I thought about my cousins Rafael and Ricardo, who a week before had terrorized me in their house. My father had taken me to visit them.

Their mother, Estela, was my father's niece. She was divorced and had four children, two girls and two boys. The boys, Rafael and Ricardo, had a pet snake that they painted in rainbow colors. After dinner my father left, and I stayed overnight with my cousins and became their target of torture. First, my two teenaged female cousins, Rosemary and Berta, locked me in their room and threw pillows at me. They laughed and then tickled me to the point that I almost urinated on their beds. When I finally managed to escape from their room, I ran into Estela, who told me, "Young man, it is time to sleep. Go with Ricardo and Rafael."

I knew then that I wouldn't be able to sleep much that night, between hearing scary stories from my cousins and their farting competition. They asked me to count to three and each of them would take turns farting as long as he could. When I refused to count any longer, they would pull me by the legs, drag me to the floor, and hit me with pillows. When the morning finally arrived, I was the first one at the table ready for breakfast, waiting for my father to return and take me home. As I departed, Estela and her children waved good-bye to me, saying, "Come back soon, so you can have a great time with us." When we were out of earshot, I hugged my father and asked him not to leave me overnight at Estela's house any-more. He didn't say a word but afterward, every time we visited Estela's house, I left with him after our visit and wished a pleasant evening to my cousins.

When my father died, my aunt Maria embraced his coffin, wailing in a voice whose tone reminded me of myself, when my father had left me that night with my cousins, "Victor, don't leave us …" Perhaps death had murmured into her ear sometime before, that soon she would have my father's name.

Aunt Maria learned how to die many times while she predicted death taking the name of people on her list. The day I learned from my mother about my aunt Maria's own death was my forty-fifth birthday. The thought of our last encounter a year before came to my mind, along with the memory of her voice saying to me, "I won't see you anymore. I won't be here when you return. Go with God, my child."

I had jokingly told her that she better wait for me because I was com-ing back for Christmas. As we looked at each other, I had felt in her visu-al embrace the sadness of knowing I would never see her again.

Among her many gifts, Aunt Maria was also a good cook. When my sis-ter Carla was a teenager, she gave her the name "Aunt Soup" because she made such great soups.

**THE UNAVOIDABLE VISITOR**

# Basic Broth

*Caldo Básica*                                                    **8 servings**

There are two different ways of preparing *caldo,* or broth. I normally sauté the meat in olive oil, letting the meat take on the flavor of the spices and the onion in the process. I prefer this method because, when the meat is sautéed first, it doesn't generate foam when the soup begins to boil. The other method is to boil the meat prior to adding any vegetables or spices.

It is important to remember to skim off any foam before the water boils. If you forget to do this, add some cold water to stop the boiling, and skim off the foam. I remember when I visited the countryside with my parents or went to see my aunt Nazaria, *caldo* was boiled at a low temperature all morning.

In some of these soups, salt is added at the end. This is the case for *quinua,* or wheat, soup. When salt is added earlier, the soup does not cook well.

Soups are also eaten with a hot sauce called *llajwa* in Quechua. This is for people who like hot spices, but is not required to appreciate the different soups. Generally speaking, Bolivian cuisine does not have too many hot, spicy foods.

| | |
|---|---|
| 1 teaspoon olive oil | 1 whole toasted white onion |
| 1 cup minced white onion | 2 carrots peeled and roughly chopped |
| 1 (3-pound) beef leg with bone, cut into 3-inch pieces | 3 sprigs parsley |
| | 1 large celery stalk |
| 1 (2-pound) leg of lamb, cut into 3-inch pieces | 1 medium tomato, halved |
| | 1 cup spinach |

Heat the oil in a skillet and sauté the onion until lightly browned. Set aside.

Bring 4 quarts water to a simmer in a pot over medium heat. Add the beef and lamb as soon as the water is warm. Skim the foam before water starts boiling.

When the water boils, add the vegetables and cook for 1 hour.

This *caldo* is the base for many Bolivian soups.

# Banana Squash Soup

This soup is primarily typical of the valley region in Bolivia, which like California is great for agriculture. I modified this soup by using banana squash rather than the traditional *zapallo* (pumpkin in Spanish) because this type of pumpkin is quite different from the pumpkins found in the U.S. Some people grow their own *zapallos* in their gardens and use the ripe vegetable to make soup. I remember eating this soup in the rainy season in Cochabamba—usually the months of February and March—which is summertime there.

| | |
|---|---|
| 1 tablespoon olive oil | ½ medium-size banana squash, peeled, seeded, and cut into 2-inch cubes |
| ½ cup minced onion | |
| 1 tablespoon minced garlic | |
| ½ teaspoon cumin | 8 small potatoes, peeled |
| 1 tablespoon dried oregano | 1 cup peas |
| ½ teaspoon salt, or to taste | ¼ cup minced fresh parsley |
| ¼ teaspoon ground black pepper | 4 avocados, peeled, pitted, halved, and sliced |
| 4 whole boneless, skinless chicken breasts, cubed | |

**60**

Heat the oil in a saucepan over medium heat, and sauté the onion and garlic until light brown and crisp. Add the cumin, oregano, salt, and pepper. Cook for 5 minutes.

Add the chicken and sauté until lightly browned. Reduce the heat to simmer and cook for 20 minutes, covered.

Add the squash. Cook for 15 minutes until the squash is soft, stirring occasionally.

Bring 3 quarts water to a boil in a pot over medium heat. Add the chicken mixture and reduce the heat to a simmer. Add more water if necessary to cover 2 inches above the mixture. Add the potatoes and cook for 40 minutes. Add the peas and cook for 15 minutes longer.

Serve in soup bowls, garnished with parsley. Add half a sliced avocado to each bowl.

# Bread Soup

This is a "dry soup" so most of the liquid is absorbed during the cooking. My aunt Maria used to make this soup, especially during the November 1 All Saints' Day (Day of the Dead) festivities. Bolivians celebrate this holiday by baking bread, and some people make good use of leftover bread in soup, like my aunt Maria did.

| | |
|---|---|
| 2 tablespoons olive oil | 1 cup chicken broth |
| 1 cup minced white onion | 4 cups diced French bread |
| 1 teaspoon minced garlic | 2 eggs, lightly beaten |
| 1 cup peeled, minced tomato | 1½ cups milk |
| 1 teaspoon minced fresh parsley | 10 thin slices *quesillo* or feta cheese |
| 1 teaspoon salt | |

Preheat the oven to 350°F. Grease an 8-inch pan.

61

Heat the oil in a saucepan over medium heat, and sauté the onion and garlic until lightly golden brown and crisp. Add the tomato, parsley, and salt. Add the chicken broth and cook for 20 minutes.

Spread a layer of bread in the prepared pan. Top with a layer of the broth mixture, a layer of *quesillo*, and then more bread. Continue layering in this order until all the ingredients are used.

In a bowl, beat the eggs and the milk together lightly before pouring over the mixture in the pan. Bake for 30 minutes. Serve hot.

# Chicken Soup

When I was growing up in Bolivia, this soup was intended for people who had colds or stomach ailments. As a kid, it was the kind of soup I enjoyed a lot because it made me feel taken care of, even when I wasn't sick.

| | |
|---|---|
| 4 whole boneless, skinless chicken breasts | ¼ teaspoon ground black pepper |
| 1 teaspoon salt | 6 medium-size potatoes, peeled |
| | 1 cup fava beans, peeled |

Wash the chicken and cut it into 2-inch cubes.

In a pot over medium heat, boil the chicken with the salt and pepper in plenty of water for 40 minutes. Add the potatoes and cook for 30 more minutes. Add the fava beans and cook for 20 additional minutes.

**62**

Serve hot.

# Chicken Soup with Vegetables

Soups are what is eaten for lunch in Bolivia, but it takes some time to make them. I learned that it can be useful to make enough soup for a few days, especially with the busy pace of life in the U.S. All you do is warm up a bowl of soup and your lunch is ready. However, this type of practicality would make eyes roll in Bolivia, where soups must be made daily using fresh vegetables.

| | |
|---|---|
| 1 tablespoon olive oil | ½ teaspoon salt, or to taste |
| ½ cup minced onion | ¼ teaspoon ground black pepper |
| 1 tablespoon minced garlic | 4 whole boneless, skinless chicken breasts, cubed |
| ½ teaspoon cumin | |
| 1 tablespoon dried oregano | 4 cups mixed raw vegetables: broccoli, carrots, and cauliflower |
| ¼ cup minced fresh parsley | |

63

Heat the oil in a pot over medium heat, and sauté the onion and garlic until light brown and crisp. Add the cumin, oregano, parsley, salt, and pepper.

Add the chicken and sauté until it is lightly browned.

Reduce the heat to a simmer and cook for 15 minutes, covered, stirring frequently so it doesn't burn.

Add approximately 8 cups boiling water to cover the mixture by 2 inches and simmer for 45 minutes. Return water to a boil and add the vegetables. Cook until the vegetables are tender.

# *Chuño* Soup

For potato soup lovers, this is a soup worth trying because the *chuño* adds a unique texture. The color of the soup will vary depending on the color of the *chuño* used.

| | |
|---|---|
| 6 cups beef broth | ½ cup fava beans, peeled |
| ½ pound boneless leg of lamb, cut in 6 pieces | ½ cup peas |
| 1 cup minced white onion | ½ teaspoon salt |
| ½ teaspoon cumin | ¼ teaspoon ground black pepper |
| ½ teaspoon dried oregano | ½ cup ground dry *chuño* (page 33), made with peeled potatoes |
| 2 large dried red chilies | 6 small potatoes, peeled |
| ¼ cup peeled, minced tomato | ¼ cup minced fresh parsley |

**64**

In a pot over medium heat, boil the lamb in the broth for 50 minutes.

Seed the dried chilies and soak in warm water until soft. Drain and squeeze dry. In a mortar and pestle or food processor, process the chilies until they form a smooth paste.

Add the onion, cumin, oregano, chili paste, tomato, fava beans, peas, salt, and pepper, and cook for 20 minutes.

Add the *chuño* slowly, stirring continuously with a wooden spoon. The soup should not stop boiling while the *chuño* is added. Continue cooking for 20 minutes.

Add the potatoes and cook for an additional 20 minutes.

Serve garnished with the parsley.

# Corn Soup

*Jak'a Lawa* is the Quechua name for corn soup. This soup is eaten during corn season, from December to March. This is summertime in Bolivia, when corn is eaten in a variety of forms from soup to *humintas* (pages 40–41). Corn is also eaten on the cob with *quesillo*. At lunchtime when this soup is served, it is common to also find the popular *choclo* on the table, a delicious big-kerneled corn much different from the sweet corn normally eaten in the U.S. *Choclo* has a different texture and is not sweet, but regular U.S. sweet corn will work in this recipe.

| | |
|---|---|
| 1 tablespoon olive oil | pieces, or 4 whole boneless, skinless |
| ½ cup minced onion | chicken breasts, cut in half |
| 1 tablespoon minced garlic | 1½ cups peeled, minced tomato |
| ½ teaspoon cumin | 5 ears corn, kernels removed and |
| ¼ teaspoon ground black pepper | ground (2¼ cups) |
| 1 tablespoon dried oregano | 8 small potatoes, halved |
| ½ teaspoon salt | ½ cup peeled fava beans or peas |
| 1 pound boneless leg of lamb, cut in 8 | ½ cup minced fresh parsley |

65

Heat the oil in a large pot over medium heat, and sauté the onion and garlic until they are light brown and crisp. Add the cumin, pepper, oregano, and salt.

Add the lamb and cook for 20 minutes. Reduce the heat to a simmer and cook the lamb for 30 minutes, covered. Continue cooking until the onion breaks down, about 10 minutes.

Add the tomato and cook until the lamb is very tender, about 1½ hours. Keep the lid on, and stir the soup occasionally.

Add the corn to the soup little by little, making sure that the water doesn't stop boiling. Let the soup boil for 10 minutes before stirring the soup. When you do begin to stir, use a wooden spoon.

This soup should be thick, but if it becomes too thick, add a little boiling water. Cook for 15 minutes.

Stir in the potatoes and the fava beans and cook until the potatoes are tender. Serve the soup garnished with parsley.

# *Cochabambina* Soup

This soup, also known as *chupe*, includes cooked wheat and seaweed. Wheat is a common ingredient in Bolivian soups. It is also toasted and eaten as a snack, known as *tostado de trigo*. Lake seaweed, known as *llul-luch'a* is another traditional ingredient. After washing, it is added to the boiling soup and cooked for 10 to 15 minutes. In the U.S. dry seaweed can be found in health food stores. This soup is typical of the Altiplano and the valley regions of Bolivia, such as Cochabamba.

| | |
|---|---|
| 1 cup *chuño* (page 33) | 1 teaspoon salt |
| 8 cups *caldo* (page 59) or water | ½ cup peas |
| ½ pound lean beef, cut in 8 pieces | ½ cup fava beans, peeled |
| ½ pound lamb, cut in 8 pieces | 4 cups peeled, julienned potatoes |
| 2 tablespoons olive oil | ½ cup peeled, sliced carrots |
| 1 cup minced white onion | ½ cup cooked hominy |
| 1 tablespoon minced garlic | ½ cup cooked wheat |
| ½ teaspoon cumin | ¼ cup dry seaweed |
| 1 teaspoon dried oregano | ¼ cup chopped green onion |
| 1 teaspoon ground red chili | 2 tablespoons minced fresh parsley |
| 1 medium tomato, peeled and chopped | |
| ½ teaspoon ground white pepper | |

Soak and peel the *chuño*, as described on page 33.

Bring the broth to a boil. Add the beef and the lamb. When the meat is cooked, strain the broth into another pot, and set the meat aside.

Heat the oil in a pan over medium heat and sauté the onion and garlic until light brown and crisp. Add the cumin, ½ teaspoon of the oregano, chili, tomato, white pepper, and salt. Pour this mixture into the broth.

Add the fava beans, peas, potatoes, and carrots, and cook for 15–20 minutes.

Add the *chuño*, cook for 15 minutes, then add the hominy and wheat. Boil the soup until the potatoes are tender. Add the seaweed 5 minutes prior to turning off the heat.

Sprinkle with the green onion, parsley, and remaining ½ teaspoon oregano and serve with a piece of beef and lamb in each bowl.

# Drunken Soup

While living in Puerto Rico, I often made this soup for a dear friend, Elmer, who loved every spoonful. He and I were new faculty members in the Communications Department at the University of the Sacred Heart. We used food to celebrate our friendship and enjoy life—very appropriate for Puerto Rico, where socializing and food are as important as salsa music. I guess I can say that a sample of my mother's kitchen left a deep impression there. This soup tastes better the next day, but won't disappoint you on the first day either.

| | |
|---|---|
| 1 tablespoon olive oil | ½ cup minced fresh parsley |
| ½ cup minced onion | ½ teaspoon salt |
| 1 tablespoon minced garlic | 1 pound sirloin tip steak, cut in 8 pieces |
| ½ teaspoon cumin | |
| ¼ teaspoon ground black pepper | 5 (12-ounce) cans light beer |
| 1 tablespoon dried oregano | 10 small potatoes |

**68**

Heat the oil in a saucepan over medium heat, and sauté the onion and garlic until light brown and crisp. Add the cumin, pepper, oregano, parsley, and salt.

Add the meat and sauté until it is almost completely cooked, cover and reduce the heat to a simmer. Continue cooking for 30 minutes, stirring often so it doesn't burn.

Add the beer to cover the meat by about 2 inches. Skim the foam created while the beer is boiling. Simmer for approximately 1½ hours. When the meat feels tender, add the potatoes. Boil the mixture until the potatoes are tender. Add water if necessary to continue to cover 2 inches above the mixture.

# Hominy Soup

This soup is from the valley region. My mother often made it for my lunch during my visits to Bolivia.

| | |
|---|---|
| 2 tablespoons olive oil | ½ teaspoon ground black pepper |
| ½ cup minced white onion | 1 tablespoon minced fresh parsley |
| 1 teaspoon minced garlic | 3 whole boneless, skinless chicken |
| ½ teaspoon dried oregano | breasts, cubed |
| 1 teaspoon salt | 1 cup hominy |

Heat the oil in a saucepan over medium heat, and sauté the onion and garlic until lightly brown and crisp. Add the oregano, salt, pepper, and parsley. Cook for 5 minutes. Add the chicken and cook for 15 minutes. Reduce the heat to a simmer. Cover and cook for about 20 minutes.

69

In a large pot over medium heat, bring 8 cups water to a boil, add the chicken mixture, and cook for 20 minutes. Add the hominy and reduce the heat to a simmer. Cook for 20 minutes until the hominy is tender.

# *Paceña* Soup

*Chuño* makes this delicious soup a must for soup lovers. Although it is also used in the valley regions of Bolivia, *chuño* is characteristic of the Altiplano region of cities such as La Paz.

½ pound sirloin tip steak, cut in 8 pieces

½ pound *charque* (page 111), cut in 8 pieces

1 teaspoon salt, or to taste

½ cup fava beans, peeled

½ cup peas

½ cup peeled, sliced carrots

4 cups peeled, julienned potatoes

1 cup prepared *chuño* (page 33)

½ cup cooked hominy

½ cup cooked wheat

2 tablespoons olive oil

½ cup minced white onion

1 teaspoon ground seeded red chili

½ teaspoon cumin

1 teaspoon dried oregano

½ teaspoon ground black pepper

¼ cup chopped green onions

1 tablespoon minced fresh parsley

1 tablespoon minced fresh mint

Bring 8 cups water to a simmer in a pot over medium heat. Add the steak and the *charque*. Skim the foam and add the salt, bring to a boil and cook for 1 hour.

Add the fava beans, peas, carrots, and potatoes, cook for 15 minutes. Add the *chuño*, cook for 5 minutes.

Add the hominy and wheat, cook until the potatoes are tender.

In a saucepan over medium heat, heat the oil and cook the onion until light brown and crisp. Add the chili, cumin, ½ teaspoon of the oregano, and the pepper. Cook for 5 minutes. Add this mixture to the meat, and cook for 10–15 minutes. Add additional water if needed, but do not let it boil over.

Remove from the heat and sprinkle with the green onions, parsley, remaining ½ teaspoon oregano, and mint.

Serve with a piece of each kind of meat.

# Peanut Soup

This soup can be found mostly in the Andes and valley regions. It is usually served with fresh, minced parsley on top. For people who love peanuts, this soup is quite simple to make and worth trying.

| | |
|---|---|
| ½ cup shelled, raw peanuts | ½ teaspoon salt |
| 2 tablespoons olive oil | 4 whole boneless, skinless chicken breasts or 2 pounds boneless lamb, cubed |
| ½ cup minced white onion | |
| 1 tablespoon minced garlic | |
| ½ teaspoon cumin | ½ cup white rice |
| ¼ teaspoon ground black pepper | ½ cup peas |
| 1 tablespoon dried oregano | 8 small potatoes, peeled |

Soak the peanuts in water overnight. The next day, remove the skins and puree the peanuts in a blender.

71

Heat the oil in a saucepan over medium heat, and sauté the onion and garlic until light brown and crisp. Add the cumin, pepper, oregano, and salt. Add the chicken and sauté until lightly browned.

Bring 10 cups of water to a boil in a pot over medium heat. Add the chicken mixture and more water if necessary to cover. Boil for 10 minutes.

Add the ground peanuts slowly. Do not stir the soup until it starts boiling again. Reduce the heat to a simmer. Use a wooden spoon to stir the soup occasionally, and cook for about 40 minutes.

Add the rice and the peas. Cook for 5 minutes and add the potatoes.

The peanut soup will be ready to serve when the potatoes are tender.

**SOUPS**

# Potato Soup with Beef

In this soup, the potatoes are mashed while raw, giving the soup a unique texture. This soup is served in the valley region of Bolivia.

| | |
|---|---|
| 1 tablespoon olive oil | ½ teaspoon salt |
| ½ cup minced onion | 1 pound sirloin tip steak, cut in 8 pieces |
| 1 tablespoon minced garlic | 12 new potatoes, peeled and mashed with a meat pounder |
| ½ teaspoon cumin | |
| ¼ teaspoon ground black pepper | 3 tablespoons minced fresh parsley |
| 1 tablespoon dried oregano | |

Heat the oil in a saucepan over medium heat, and sauté the onion and garlic until light brown and crisp. Add the cumin, pepper, oregano, parsley and salt and cook for 5–10 minutes.

Add the meat and sauté until it is almost cooked. Cover and reduce the heat to simmer. Stir the ingredients often so they won't burn. Continue cooking for 30 minutes.

Add water to cover the meat by about 2 inches and cook for 1½ hours, or until the meat is tender. Return to a boil and add the mashed potatoes. Boil until the potatoes are tender. You may need to add more water to keep the meat covered by 2 inches.

Garnish each soup bowl with parsley.

**MY MOTHER'S BOLIVIAN KITCHEN**

72

# Quinoa Soup

Quinoa is a grain typical of the Andes region and these days can be found in most health food stores in the U.S. It is nutritious and can be cooked in a number of ways, including in soups.

| | |
|---|---|
| 2 large dried red or yellow chilies | 1 pound boneless lamb, cut in 8 pieces |
| 2 tablespoons olive oil | ¾ cup quinoa (see Note) |
| ½ cup minced white onion | ½ cup peas |
| 1 tablespoon minced garlic | ½ cup fava beans, peeled |
| ½ teaspoon cumin | 8 small red potatoes, peeled |
| ½ teaspoon dried oregano | ½ teaspoon salt |
| ½ teaspoon ground white pepper | 2 tablespoons minced fresh parsley |

In a large pot over medium heat, bring 8 cups of water to a boil.

In the meantime, seed the chilies and soak in warm water until soft. Drain and squeeze dry. In a mortar and pestle or food processor, process the chilies until they form a smooth paste.

73

Heat the oil in a saucepan over medium heat, and sauté the onion and garlic until light brown and crisp. Add the cumin, oregano, pepper, and chili paste. Cook for 5 minutes.

Add the lamb and sauté until browned and almost cooked.

Add the lamb mixture to the boiling water. Add more water if necessary, to cover, and return to a boil. Cook for 15 minutes.

Add the quinoa and continue cooking for 1 hour. Add the peas, fava beans, potatoes, and salt, and cook until the potatoes are tender.

Serve the quinoa soup garnished with parsley.

**Note:** If you bought the quinoa in a box, you don't need to wash it before using it. Bulk quinoa, however, sometimes contains small stones and should be rinsed thoroughly.

It is important to add salt only after the quinoa is cooked, otherwise the quinoa won't cook properly.

**SOUPS**

# Baked Rice Soup

This soup, baked in the oven, is like a savory rice pudding. The cheese melts into the rice, creating a delicious concoction.

| | |
|---|---|
| ½ teaspoon dried oregano | 1 tablespoon minced fresh parsley |
| 1 teaspoon salt | ½ cup chicken broth |
| 2 cups white rice | 2 eggs, lightly beaten |
| 2 tablespoons olive oil | 6 slices *quesillo* or feta cheese |
| ½ cup minced white onion | 2 hard-boiled eggs, each sliced into 6 pieces |
| ½ cup peeled, minced tomato | |
| ½ teaspoon ground black pepper | 6 black olives, pitted and halved |

In a pot over medium heat, combine 4 cups water, the oregano, salt, and rice, and bring to a boil. Reduce the heat to a simmer and cook for 15–20 minutes. Remove from the heat and set aside.

**74**

Preheat the oven to 350°F. Grease an 8-inch pan.

In a pot over medium heat, heat 1 tablespoon of the oil and fry the onion until light brown and crisp. Add the tomato, pepper, parsley, and broth. Cook for 15 minutes and remove from the heat.

Mix the eggs into the rice mixture.

Pour half of the rice evenly into the prepared pan. On top, evenly layer half the onion mixture, and all of the *quesillo*, the hard-boiled eggs, and the olives. Spread the rest of the rice on top, then the remainder of the onion mixture. Bake for 15 minutes.

Cut into six slices and serve hot.

# Stuffed Rice Soup

This is another dry soup, which is a popular dish in South America.

| Rice: | Stuffing: |
|---|---|
| ½ teaspoon salt | 2 tablespoons olive oil |
| 2 cups white rice | ½ cup minced white onion |
| | ¼ cup peeled, minced tomato |
| | ½ teaspoon ground black pepper |
| | ½ teaspoon salt |
| | 3 boneless skinless chicken breasts, cut into 2-inch cubes |
| | ½ cup chicken broth |
| | 1 hard-boiled egg, diced |
| | 6 black olives, pitted and halved |

75

Bring 8 cups water to a boil in a pot over medium heat, and add the salt and rice. Reduce the heat to a simmer and cook for 30 minutes. Remove from the heat and set aside.

**For the stuffing:** Heat 1 tablespoon of the oil in a pot over medium heat, and sauté the onion until light brown and crisp. Add the tomato, pepper, salt, chicken, and broth. Cook for 15 minutes and remove from the heat. Stir in the hard-boiled egg.

Heat 1½ teaspoons of the remaining oil in a saucepan over medium heat. Add half of the rice mixture to the pan, spreading evenly. Add the olives and the onion mixture, and cover with the remaining rice. Shaking the pan to prevent sticking, cook for 4 minutes. Cover the saucepan with a lid and gently invert the rice onto it. Into the same saucepan, pour the remaining 1½ teaspoons of oil and gently tip the rice back into the saucepan on the uncooked side. Cook for 2 minutes.

Cut into six slices and serve hot.

# Spaghetti Soup

This is a popular soup served for lunch in most regions of Bolivia.

| | |
|---|---|
| ½ pound lamb shoulder, cut into 2-inch cubes | ½ cup peeled, chopped tomatoes |
| 1 large dried red or yellow chili | 10 ounces spaghetti |
| 2 tablespoons olive oil | ½ cup fava beans, peeled |
| ½ cup minced white onion | ½ cup peas |
| 1 tablespoon minced garlic | 1 teaspoon salt |
| ½ teaspoon cumin | 8 potatoes, peeled and quartered |
| ½ teaspoon ground white pepper | 2 tablespoons minced fresh parsley |
| 1½ teaspoons dried oregano | |

In a pot over medium heat, bring 10 cups water to a boil. Add the lamb and cook until tender. Drain and set aside.

Seed the chili and soak in warm water until soft. Drain and squeeze dry. In a mortar and pestle or food processor, process the chili until a smooth paste forms.

Heat the olive oil in a saucepan over medium heat, and sauté the onion and garlic until light brown and crisp. Add the cumin, white pepper, ½ teaspoon of the oregano, and chili paste. Cook for 3 minutes.

Add the lamb to the onion mixture and cook for 5 minutes. Add the tomato and cook for 20 minutes, stirring occasionally with a wooden spoon.

Bring 10 cups of water to a boil in a large pot over medium heat and stir in the lamb mixture. Cook for 10 minutes and add the spaghetti, fava beans, peas, and salt. Reduce the heat to a simmer and continue cooking for about 1 hour.

Add the potatoes and cook for 20 more minutes, or until tender.

Remove the soup from the heat and garnish with parsley and the remaining 1 teaspoon of oregano before serving.

# Wheat Soup

Soup is the main component of any Bolivian lunch and this tasty preparation can be served any day or season of the year. This soup is prepared particularly in the Altiplano and valley regions of the country.

| | |
|---|---|
| 1½ cups wheat | ½ teaspoon dried oregano |
| ½ pound *charque* (page111), cut in 6 pieces | ¼ teaspoon ground black pepper |
| 1 pound boneless leg of lamb, cut in 6 pieces | 2 teaspoons minced garlic |
| 2 large dried red chilies | 1 teaspoon salt |
| ½ cup minced white onion | 4 small potatoes, peeled and quartered |
| ½ teaspoon cumin | ½ cup fava beans, peeled |
| | ½ cup peas |
| | 2 tablespoons minced fresh parsley |

In a pot over medium heat, toast the wheat for about 10 minutes. In a mortar and pestle or food processor, grind the wheat until finely ground.

Bring 8 cups of water to a boil in a pot over medium heat, and add the *charque* and the lamb. Cook for 30 minutes.

In the meantime, seed the dried chilies and soak in warm water until soft. Drain and squeeze dry. In a mortar and pestle or food processor, process the chilies until they form a smooth paste.

Add the onion, cumin, oregano, pepper, garlic, chili paste, and salt to the meat. Cook for 15 minutes.

In a bowl, mix the ground wheat with 1¼ cups water and slowly add it to the boiling soup. Cook for 20 minutes, stirring occasionally to dissolve the wheat.

Add the potatoes, fava beans, and peas. Cook for 20 more minutes, until the potatoes are tender.

Garnish with parsley and serve.

# AUNT NAZARIA'S BIRTHDAY

Early on the morning of January 12, 1957, preparations to go to my aunt Nazaria's sixty-ninth birthday party are under way. As usual, everyone in my family is busy, taking a shower or getting dressed. In my room, I put on the new shirt I was given for the occasion. I can hear my mother telling my sisters to hurry up while they put on their dresses. I put on my black shorts with suspenders and look for my socks in the drawer where I keep my underwear. After I am completely dressed, I lie down on the bed with my hands behind my head, and look at my laced black

shoes. My eyes seem to go into motion as my head tilts toward the ceiling. I give a strong sigh as I imagine eating at Aunt Nazaria's house. My thoughts are interrupted and vanish like smoke when I hear my mother's voice, "Son, are you coming?"

I see my mother standing at the door, looking at me and holding the door with her left hand. I jump from bed and say, "Yes!"

When I think about my mother, the first image that comes to mind is the expression in her eyes. They had a mixture of sadness and peacefulness at the same time, which seemed to hold the passages of her life. At an early age, she lost both of her parents and was reared by her grandmother. I remember some of the pictures that my father took of her when they first met; my sister Carla's beauty reminds me of her.

I feel the touch of her left hand on my right shoulder as I pass by her, still standing at the door. Her beauty remains engraved in the stroll of time, along with her grace.

Aunt Nazaria lived in the countryside, where she had a big farmhouse by the Rocha River. She had animals, including cows, sheep, chicken, ducks, geese, and turkeys. She also grew potatoes and vegetables on her land. She lived with her maids and some people who helped her with the land as well the house. She had seven children—five sons and two daughters—who were all married and had their own families.

Her house had many rooms that all faced a central patio. The kitchen was near her bedroom and didn't have a modern stove, so it took time to prepare food. The maids cooked the food under Aunt Nazaria's supervision, using copper and clay pots with wooden spoons that hung from a big piece of wood above the adobe stove. The kitchen was painted white, like most of the adobe house. I used to sit and observe the cooking process that took place in that busy world where the fire in the kitchen never seemed to rest, always jumping up and down with its colorful flames. The maids sat around the kitchen peeling potatoes, cutting vegetables, and boiling water for tea, the voices of their conversation joining the noise made by the movement of the utensils.

That day of my aunt's birthday, the kitchen is my second stop after greeting her. When I greet her, she gives me a joyful spank on my behind. As I walk toward the kitchen pots, I am greeted warmly by the cooks, a group of women, young and old. What I enjoy most about being there is that they let me test the food to see what I think about it. The big wooden spoon in front of my face holds a piece of duck. At the end of the arm holding the spoon is Doña Alicia, inclining her face slightly toward her right shoulder as she asks if I want some: *"¿Quieres un poquito?"*

Two younger cooks stop their routine to smile and await my reaction. The others glance at me and continue their work. My fingers seem to answer first as they hurry to grab the steaming white meat cooked in a sauce of the mild yellow pepper we call *aji amarillo*. After tasting the delicious duck, I know dinner that evening will be *picante de pato con chuño*. I look into the pot where the cooks are boiling the *chuño* and I notice the hand of one of the other cooks is stirring finely chopped onions in a pan with olive oil. She looks at me without lifting her face, and asks me about my taste of duck, *"¿Rico?"*

My mouth is still full, so all I can do is groan a positive response. Afterward, I see the same cook pouring eggs and cheese into the frying pan. The aromas in the kitchen switch to another delicious smell of a condiment called *ahogado*. The *ahogado* is stirred into the cooked *chuño*, until I hear one of the voices say, *"Listo."*

Half an hour later, I am served a ceramic plate full of *chuño* and duck cooked with *aji amarillo*, as well as a big potato that continues to steam in front of my eyes. I eat dinner next to my mother at a table that seems so large, I have no idea where it ends. Sometimes, I think that my aunt performed miracles like those mentioned in the bible, the ones where Jesus fed people by performing miracles. This time, I believe the miracle is performed with *picante de pato con chuño*, rather than fish and bread. I notice that the plates keep coming out of the kitchen until everyone has a dish in front of his nose.

After we eat, I play games with two of my younger cousins, Miguel and Ivette. They are siblings, the children of my father's nephew, whose name is also Miguel. We walk around the river and look for things to pick up, like flowers or rocks, and simply get reacquainted with each other. My aunt's birthday is a family get-together where all the families gather for a week to eat and celebrate. There aren't many other occasions where we have the opportunity to do this.

Aunt Nazaria's gray hair and the wrinkles on her face contrast with her small body, which moves with the energy of a young woman. There is something peculiar about her body expressions, one in particular, which I like to watch. When she walks, she stops and turns around and, as she does this, she puts her left hand on her hip and looks in the direction where her eyes lead her. Sometimes her eyes find me looking at her, and we exchange glittering smiles. My aunt is a widow whose husband died many years before I had a chance to meet him. She keeps a photograph of him by her bedside, in which the two of them look straight at the camera, frozen in time in a sepia-color image.

For her birthday celebration, almost fifty relatives have converged on her house. The adults eat, drink, talk, dance to a live band, and sleep. The children have the pleasurable task of observing the adults' behavior at the party, which, I must say, is always fun. My sister Carla imitates the adults back home, sometimes at the dinner table under the disapproving faces of my parents, who in the end have no choice but to laugh like the rest of us. Carla is particularly good at imitating Aunt Nazaria and a cousin nicknamed "Chicken Soup." His real name is Patricio, but he got the "Chicken Soup" moniker because one time he got drunk at my aunt's birthday party and made a fool of himself, saying he only wanted chicken soup for lunch. This gave my teenaged sister enough comedy material to use until my aunt's next birthday.

Since there are so many of us at my aunt's house, each family sleeps in a room allocated to them. I believe Nazaria has the biggest bed in her bedroom, because the other beds in her house are not that wide. My two sisters, Guichy and Carla (my younger sister Mary was not born yet), my parents, and I sleep in the same room, which has three beds. I usually end up sleeping at the foot of one of the beds. This is not a problem except that my parents' snoring goes all night long. I close my eyes and try to sleep, but Carla's voice bounces in the dark room saying, "Should I wake you up for auntie's performance tonight?"

To which I say, "Oh no!"

Later that night, Aunt Nazaria wakes up nearly everyone in the house, singing in her loud, drunken voice. She passionately sings a popular political song in Quéchua: "Do not let Martin Lanza die when he is sent to Quintanilla..." The song is one to which my sister Carla had ascribed a sexual meaning the previous year. Carla can't stop laughing while my aunt goes on unaware of her niece's lewd interpretation of the lyrics: "Don't do it to me that way. Don't do it to me that way. You are going to hurt me. Oh my dear Martin Lanza, my beloved companion!"

The smell of fresh bread baked in the adobe oven wakes me the next morning. I go out to the patio and realize I am the only one there besides the people baking the bread. As I get ready for breakfast, one of the cooks places a hot cup of tea made from the skin of cacao beans for me on the kitchen table along with the "biblical bread." This is the name Carla and I gave the big, round bread with cheese that my aunt had her cooks bake every day for breakfast. That morning, my eyes gaze at the guitars and saxophones left sitting on some of the chairs and I see Aunt Nazaria mimic a dance in the middle of the patio as she looks and waves at me. I wave back at her with the cup of hot tea in my right hand and a piece of warm bread in my mouth.

# Chicken with Banana Squash

*Pollo con Calabaza*                    **6 servings**

This is a soup that pumpkin lovers will appreciate for its taste and nutrition. In Bolivia soups are made daily and never served as leftovers. However, I managed to break that tradition and now make this soup to be eaten for several days. I find that it tastes even better the next day when warmed up for lunch. This soup is typical of the state of Cochabamba.

| | |
|---|---|
| 2 tablespoons olive oil | ½ teaspoon salt |
| 1 teaspoon minced garlic | ½ teaspoon ground black pepper |
| 1 cup minced white onion | 1 banana or other winter squash, |
| 4 whole boneless, skinless chicken breasts, diced into 2-inch cubes | peeled and cut into 1-inch pieces |
| | 1 cup fresh shelled soybeans |

Heat the oil in a large frying pan over medium heat, and cook the garlic until fragrant. Add the onion and sauté until crisp and light brown.

Stir in the chicken, salt, and pepper. Cook, covered, for 30 minutes until a sauce forms. Add the squash and cook until tender, about 20 minutes.

In a pot over medium heat, bring 8 cups water to a boil. Add the chicken mixture and bring it back to a boil, then add the soybeans. Continue cooking until the soybeans are tender, about 10 minutes.

# Chicken with Beets

This dish is from the region of Cochabamba, an agricultural state where it is easy to find a great variety of vegetables, including beets. It is simple to make and all the ingredients can be easily found in the U.S.

| | |
|---|---|
| 4 whole boneless, skinless chicken breasts | 4 potatoes, peeled |
| ½ teaspoon salt | 4 medium-size beets, peeled |
| ½ teaspoon ground black pepper | 2 tablespoons olive oil |

Place the chicken in a pot, cover with water. Add the salt and black pepper, and bring to a boil over medium heat. Cook for 30 minutes. Add the potatoes and cook until tender. Drain and let cool.

**84**

In a separate pot over medium heat, cook the beets in boiling water until tender. Young beets take 30 minutes to 1 hour to cook. Older beets take 1 to 2 hours. Drain and julienne the beets. Toss the beets with the oil and season to taste with additional salt and pepper.

In a saucepan over medium heat, sauté the chicken until golden brown.

Serve each person one chicken breast and one potato, with the beets.

# Chicken with Carrots

This dish was one of my favorites when I was a child. I liked the smell of the carrots and the sauce made by my mother. This dish also reminds me of the experience I had in the northern part of the state of Potosi when I witnessed the *tinku* ritual (page 9). This dish was known by my mother and me as "chicken a la señorita," or *pollo a la señorita* in Spanish because as a child, when I tried to pronounce *zanahorita* (little carrot) it came out sounded like *señorita*.

| | |
|---|---|
| 6 whole boneless, skinless chicken breasts | 4 cups peeled, sliced carrots |
| 4 green onions, whole | 3 tablespoons olive oil |
| 1 tablespoon minced garlic | ½ cup minced white onion |
| ½ teaspoon salt | ½ cup peeled, chopped tomato |
| ½ teaspoon ground black pepper | 3 eggs, lightly beaten |
| 8 medium-size potatoes, peeled | 1 cup crumbled feta cheese |

85

In a pot over medium heat, add water to cover the chicken and cook for 45 minutes. Add the green onions, garlic, salt, and pepper. Drain, set aside, and let cool.

In another pot over medium heat, cook the potatoes in boiling water until tender, without overcooking them. Drain and set aside. In a separate pot, steam the carrots until tender.

In a dry saucepan over medium heat, sauté the chicken on both sides until it acquires a golden color.

In a pot over medium heat, heat the oil and cook the onion until golden and crispy. Add the tomato and cook for 5 minutes, stirring constantly. Add the eggs and cook the sauce for another 3 minutes, stirring constantly. Stir the feta cheese into the sauce and mix the sauce with the carrots. Serve the chicken and potatoes with the sauce on the side.

# Chicken *Ch'anqa*

This typical dish from the state of Cochabamba is usually served for lunch. The following recipe indicates to drain the cooking liquid, however, you can disregard this step and serve it as a soup.

| | |
|---|---|
| ½ teaspoon salt | 3 cups fava beans, peeled |
| 6 whole boneless, skinless chicken breasts | 1½ cups green onion, chopped into 1-inch pieces |
| 6 potatoes, peeled and halved | |

In a pot, bring 6 cups water to a boil and then add the salt and the chicken. Cook for about 30 minutes.

Add the potatoes and cook for 20 more minutes.

Add the fava beans and cook for 15 additional minutes, until the potatoes are tender.

Five minutes before serving, add the green onions. Drain the cooking liquid without stirring the ingredients.

Serve with *uchu llajwa* (yellow chili sauce) (page 14) spooned on top of each serving.

# Chicken with Corn

The type of corn used in this dish is not sweet corn but has bigger kernels and is not that juicy. Mexican white corn is similar to the white corn used in Bolivia and may be used as a substitute in this recipe.

| | |
|---|---|
| 2 tablespoons olive oil | 4 whole boneless, skinless chicken breasts, diced |
| 1 cup minced white onion | 7 ears corn |
| 1 teaspoon minced garlic | 1 cup evaporated milk |
| 1 red bell pepper, sliced | 1 tablespoon sugar |
| 2 tablespoons minced fresh parsley | 1 teaspoon butter |
| ½ teaspoon salt | |

Heat the oil in a pan over medium heat, and sauté the onion, garlic, red pepper, parsley, and salt. Add the chicken and fry until light brown.

Remove the kernels from five ears of corn. In a mortar and pestle or with a food processor, grind the corn until it forms a smooth paste. Grate the other two ears of corn with a cheese grater.

In a pot over medium heat, heat the evaporated milk, ground and grated corn, chicken mixture, sugar, and butter. Cook over medium-low heat for 30 minutes, stirring frequently, until the chicken is cooked through. Add more evaporated milk if the sauce reduces too much while cooking.

Serve hot.

# Chicken with Cream

The creamy lemon flavor of this dish adds up to a delightful chicken variation.

| | |
|---|---|
| 6 whole boneless, skinless chicken breasts | 2 tablespoons butter, melted |
| Juice of 1 lemon | 2 cups heavy cream |
| ½ teaspoon salt | 6 potatoes, peeled |
| ½ teaspoon ground black pepper | 2 cups peas |

Preheat the oven to 350°F.

Place the chicken in a pan and add the lemon juice, salt, pepper, and 1 tablespoon of the butter, and bake for 30 minutes, or until cooked through.

**88**

In a large pot over medium heat, melt the remaining 1 tablespoon of butter and pour in the cream little by little without stirring. Do not let it boil; remove from the heat when it is heated through.

Add the baked chicken to the cream mixture. Continue cooking over medium-low heat for 10 minutes.

Boil the potatoes and steam peas separately, and serve with the chicken.

# Chicken Fricassee

*Fricasé* can also be prepared with regular milk, but I prefer to use evaporated milk because it gives a richer flavor to this dish. *Fricasé* is usually prepared in the valley and Altiplano regions of Bolivia.

| | |
|---|---|
| 4 whole boneless, skinless chicken breasts | 1 cup peas |
| 1 cup evaporated milk | 1 cup sliced asparagus |
| 1 tablespoon butter | 1 tablespoon cornstarch |
| 1 teaspoon salt | 4 potatoes, boiled |

Bring water to a boil in a pot over medium heat, and poach the chicken. Reserve ¼ cup of the cooking liquid. Drain and shred the chicken into bite-size pieces.

In a pot over medium heat, heat the evaporated milk, butter, salt, and reserved poaching liquid. Add the peas, and the asparagus; bring the mixture to a boil, then reduce the heat to a simmer. Mix the cornstarch with ½ cup cold water, and stir it into the milk mixture. Add the chicken and continue cooking for 20 to 30 minutes, until the vegetables are tender.

Serve with the potatoes.

# Chicken in Orange-Wine Sauce

The wine and orange juice in this recipe adds a tangy flavor to the chicken and makes this a good meal to prepare for friends and family.

| | |
|---|---|
| 2 tablespoons olive oil | 6 whole boneless, skinless chicken breasts, diced |
| 1 cup minced white onion | ¼ cup raisins |
| 1 teaspoon minced garlic | 1 (15-ounce) can tomato sauce |
| ½ teaspoon salt | 2 cups orange juice |
| ½ teaspoon ground black pepper | ½ cup white wine |

**90**

Heat the oil in a large frying pan over medium heat, and sauté the onion, garlic, salt, and pepper. Add the chicken and sauté until light brown.

Add the remaining ingredients and cook over medium-low heat for 30 minutes, until the chicken is cooked through and a sauce forms.

Serve with salad, potatoes, and rice.

# Chicken *Sajta*

*Sajta* mean "delicacy" in Quechua. *Sajta de pollo* can be prepared either for lunch or dinner. It is frequently made when friends and relatives visit as a way of welcoming them. This dish is from the Altiplano and valley regions of Bolivia.

| | |
|---|---|
| 8 dried yellow chilies | 4 whole boneless, skinless chicken breasts |
| 5 green onions | 1 large carrot, peeled |
| 2 tablespoons minced garlic | 4 potatoes, peeled |
| ½ cup olive oil | 2 cups fava beans, peeled |

Seed the chilies and soak them in warm water until soft. Drain and squeeze dry.

In a blender or food processor, process the green part of three of the green onions, garlic, oil, and chilies. Pulse in several bursts until well mixed, but not a smooth paste. Cook the mixture in a pot over medium heat for about 7–10 minutes.

Chop the remaining green onions and the carrots.

Bring a pot of water to a boil over medium heat, and poach the chicken, with the carrot and green onions.

In two separate pots, boil the potatoes and the fava beans until tender.

Combine the chicken with the chili mixture and top with the cooked fava beans.

Serve with the potatoes on the side.

# Chicken Salad

This dish is usually eaten in bars when people gather to discuss politics, sports, or simply to play the popular dice game known as *cacho*.

| | |
|---|---|
| 2 whole boneless, skinless chicken breasts, poached | 1 cup diced, cooked potatoes |
| 1 tablespoon white wine vinegar | 1 cup peas, cooked |
| 1 tablespoon olive oil | ½ cup minced white onion |
| ½ teaspoon salt, or to taste | ½ cup peeled, chopped tomato |
| ½ teaspoon ground black pepper | 2 hard-boiled eggs, sliced |
| 1 cup diced, cooked carrots | 3 cups finely chopped lettuce |

Cut the chicken into 2-inch strips. In a skillet over medium heat, heat the oil and sauté the chicken until well browned. Remove the chicken from the heat and chill.

Toss the chilled chicken with the vinegar and oil, and add salt and pepper a little at a time, tasting for seasoning. Mix the carrots, potatoes, peas, onion, tomato, eggs, and lettuce with the chicken and serve.

# Chicken Sautéed in Wine

*Gallina Frita en Vino*                                          **4 servings**

The state of Tarija produces some good, very inexpensive wines, which can be used for drinking or making this dish. However, you don't have to be in Tarija to make this dish; there are plenty of wines in the U.S. that you can use in this recipe. It is certainly a good meal after a long day at work.

| | |
|---|---|
| 2 tablespoons olive oil | 4 whole boneless, skinless chicken breasts |
| 2 tablespoons minced garlic | |
| 1 cup thinly sliced mushrooms | 2 tablespoons flour |
| ½ cup white wine | 2 tablespoons minced fresh parsley |

Heat the oil in a pan over medium heat, and cook the garlic until fragrant.

Stir in the mushrooms and wine, and cook for 2 to 5 minutes. Dust the chicken with the flour and sauté until cooked through.

Transfer the chicken to a plate and garnish with the minced parsley. Serve with salad or vegetables and potatoes.

# Chicken Stew

Foods and smells are associated with places and memories. This dish reminds me of rainy days, which in Bolivia happen during summertime. I remember having this meal after coming home from elementary school in the afternoon and the steamy smell of my dinner coming to the table on a warm plate.

| | |
|---|---|
| 4 whole boneless, skinless chicken breasts | ½ teaspoon salt |
| 2 tablespoons olive oil | ½ teaspoon ground black pepper |
| 1 cup minced white onion | 4 small potatoes, peeled |
| ½ cup minced tomato | 1 cup peas |
| 3 medium-size carrots, peeled and cut into 1-inch pieces | 2 tablespoons white vinegar |
| ½ cup minced fresh parsley | 1 egg white |

**94**

In a pot over medium heat, heat the oil and sauté the chicken until almost cooked through.

Reduce the heat to low and add 2 cups water, the onion, tomato, carrots, parsley, salt, and pepper. Simmer for 30 minutes. Add the potatoes and cook until tender. Add the peas and cook for 5 additional minutes. Add ½ cup water if the mixture is too dry.

Five minutes prior to serving, mix the vinegar with the egg white and stir into the stew.

Serve the dish with toasted rice (page 47).

# Fried Chicken with Cream

*Pollo Frito en Crema*                                     **6 servings**

The tasty spiced cream sauce is a good combination with the eggs and potato.

| | |
|---|---|
| 2 tablespoons olive oil | 1 bell pepper, sliced |
| 1 cup chopped white onion | 2 cups heavy cream |
| 1 teaspoon minced garlic | 6 potatoes |
| ½ teaspoon salt | 6 hard-boiled eggs, sliced |
| ½ teaspoon ground black pepper | |
| 6 whole boneless, skinless chicken breasts, diced | |

Heat the oil in a pan over medium heat, and sauté the onion, garlic, salt, and pepper. Add the chicken and sauté until light brown. Add the bell pepper. Continue cooking, covered, over medium-low heat for 25 minutes. This mixture will generate its own sauce.

In a small saucepan over medium heat, heat the cream with 2 tablespoons of the liquid from the chicken pan. Remove from the heat when the cream mixture is warm. Do not let it boil.

Boil the potatoes separately.

To serve, pour the cream sauce over the chicken. Garnish with hard-boiled eggs and serve the potatoes on the side.

# Chicken with Yucca

Pastel de Pollo con Yuca                                    6 servings

*Yuca*, a potato-like root, is mainly used in the states of Pando, Beni, and Santa Cruz. However, *yuca* can also be found in the valley regions of Bolivia, such as the state of Cochabamba. When I cook this for friends unfamiliar with *yuca*, they love it. *Yuca* is available in most supermarkets in large cities.

| | |
|---|---|
| 2 medium-size yuccas | ½ teaspoon salt |
| 2 tablespoons butter | ½ teaspoon ground black pepper |
| 2 cups evaporated milk | 2 cups peas |
| 6 whole boneless, skinless chicken breasts | 1 egg |
| 2 tablespoons cornstarch | |

Peel the yucca and cut it into 2-inch pieces. Make sure to remove the fibrous core.

In a pot over medium heat bring water to a boil. Cook the yucca for 20 minutes until almost tender. Do not overcook or the pieces will fall apart and become mushy. Drain and set aside. Mash the yucca with 1 tablespoon of the butter and 1½ cups of the evaporated milk.

In a pot over medium heat, bring water to a boil and poach the chicken until it is cooked through. Drain and shred the chicken into 1-inch pieces.

Preheat the oven to 350°F. Grease an 8-inch pan.

96

Dissolve the cornstarch in ½ cup cold water. In a large saucepan, combine the cornstarch mixture, the remaining ½ cup of evaporated milk, remaining 1 tablespoon of butter, salt, and pepper. Add the peas and the shredded chicken, and bring the mixture to a boil. Reduce the heat to low, and cook until the peas are almost tender, about 3 minutes.

Spread half of the mashed yucca in the prepared pan and smooth the surface. Add the chicken mixture in an even layer. Pour the other half of the yucca on top of the chicken filling.

Beat the egg and use a pastry brush to paint the top layer of the yucca.

Bake the *pastel* for 20 minutes, or until the surface is golden brown.

Slice the *pastel* and serve warm.

# Meat-Stuffed Chicken

A combination of meats is typical of several Bolivian dishes including *pollo relleno de carnes*. This combination gives a unique, delightful taste.

| | |
|---|---|
| 2 tablespoons butter | 1 cup cubed whole wheat bread |
| ¼ pound pork tenderloin, cut into 1-inch cubes | ¼ cup sliced Spanish olives |
| ¼ pound beef, cut into 1-inch cubes | ½ teaspoon ground black pepper |
| ¾ cup evaporated milk | 1 cup sliced apples, such as Granny Smith |
| 2 ounces pâté, any kind | 1 raw egg |
| ½ cup chopped prunes | 1 (4-pound) chicken |
| ¼ cup sliced almonds | 2 hard-boiled eggs |

Preheat the oven to 350°F.

**98**

Melt 1 tablespoon of the butter in a pan over medium heat, and sauté the pork and beef until cooked through. Add the evaporated milk, pâté, prunes, almonds, bread, olives, pepper, apples, and the raw egg. Bring the mixture to a boil.

Place the chicken in a baking dish. Put the two hard-boiled eggs inside the chicken. Stuff the meat mixture into the chicken, and sew the cavity closed. Smear the chicken with the remaining 1 tablespoon of butter.

Bake the chicken for approximately 1½ hours.

# Spicy Chicken

This is a popular dish in Bolivia and can be found in most states. Although the word *picante* means spicy in Spanish, the dish can be adjusted for different tastes. My mother didn't include the seeds of the chili therefore her *picante de pollo* didn't entirely live up to its name. Serrano or California chilies can be substituted for the Bolivian chilies. This dish is traditionally served with *chuño phuti*, sautéed freeze-dried potatoes. You can also add a tomato salsa to the *chuño*.

| | |
|---|---|
| 7 large dry red chilies, seeded | ½ teaspoon salt |
| 2 tablespoons olive oil | ½ teaspoon ground black pepper |
| 2 cups minced white onion | 1 cup minced tomato |
| 2 teaspoons minced garlic | 1 cup peas |
| 6 whole boneless, skinless chicken breasts | 6 peeled potatoes, boiled |
| | *Chuño phuti* (page 34) |
| 1 tablespoon cumin | *Salsa cruda* (page 32) |
| 1 tablespoon dried oregano | ½ cup minced fresh parsley |

99

Soak the chilies in warm water until soft. Drain and squeeze out excess water. In a mortar and pestle or food processor, process the chilies until they form a smooth paste.

In a pan over medium heat, heat the oil and sauté the onion with the garlic until crisp and light brown. Add the chicken, cumin, oregano, chili paste, salt, and pepper, and cook for about 15 minutes. Add the tomato and peas. Stir to mix well, and bring to a boil. Reduce the heat to low and simmer for 1 hour, until the chicken is cooked through. Add 1 tablespoon hot water if the juices evaporate.

Serve with a potato per person, a portion of *chuño phuti* with *salsa cruda* on top. Garnish with parsley.

# *Pavita* Sandwich

Although in Spanish the word *pavita* means "little female turkey," this sandwich includes chicken. In the 1960s this sandwich was quite popular in Bolivia as something people ate with a soda after going to the movies at night. It is very easy to prepare and makes a good lunch. While living in Puerto Rico, I discovered adobo, a blend of seasonings, garlic, oregano, and salt. This all-purpose seasoning can be found in most supermarkets across the United States and I use it when boiling the chicken.

| | |
|---|---|
| 3 whole boneless, skinless chicken breasts | 2 tablespoons mayonnaise |
| ½ teaspoon salt | 12 slices bread |
| ¼ teaspoon ground black pepper | 3 avocados, peeled, pitted, and sliced |
| | 1 cup cashews (optional) |

**100**

In a pot over medium heat, poach the chicken with the salt and pepper until tender. Drain and let cool.

Shred the chicken and mix it with the mayonnaise.

To assemble the sandwiches: divide the chicken among six slices of bread. Top with ½ an avocado and a small amount of cashews. Top each sandwich with another slice of bread.

The chicken can also be served without bread, with vegetables, such as carrots.

# Chicken Pie with Potato

Potatoes are consumed daily by Bolivians in one way or another. This meal combines two ingredients commonly used—potatoes and chicken. The variety of potatoes in Bolivia is quite large compared to most countries and the type of potato traditionally used for this recipe is called *runa*, Quechua for "man". It is round, medium-sized, white and has a unique floury texture. This dish can, however, be easily made in the U.S. because any type of potato can be used.

| | |
|---|---|
| 2 pounds potatoes, peeled and sliced | ½ teaspoon salt |
| 2 tablespoons butter | ½ teaspoon ground black pepper |
| 2 cups evaporated milk | 2 cups peas |
| 6 whole boneless, skinless chicken breasts | 1 egg |
| 2 tablespoons cornstarch | |

Place the potatoes in a pot and add water to cover. Bring to a boil and cook until tender. Mash the potatoes with 1 tablespoon of the butter and 1½ cups of the evaporated milk.

In a pot, bring water to a boil and poach the chicken until it is cooked through. Drain and shred the chicken into 1-inch pieces.

Preheat the oven to 350°F. Grease an 8-inch pan.

Dissolve the cornstarch in cold water. In a large saucepan, combine the cornstarch mixture with the remaining ½ cup of evaporated milk, remaining 1 tablespoon butter, salt, and pepper. Add the peas and the shredded chicken. Bring the mixture to a boil, then reduce the heat to a simmer. Cook until the peas are almost tender, about 3 minutes.

Spread half of the potato mixture into the prepared pan and smooth the surface. Add the chicken mixture in an even layer. Pour the other half of the potato mixture on top of the chicken filling.

Beat the egg and use a pastry brush to paint the top layer of potato. Bake the *pastel* for 20 minutes, or until the surface is golden brown.

Slice the *pastel* and serve warm.

**POULTRY**

# Corn Pastry with Chicken Stuffing

This dish is similar to *huminta al horno,* with the exception that it is filled with more than *quesillo* cheese. It is prepared during summertime when fresh corn is available. To make this recipe, white corn with large kernels, rather than sweet corn generally found across the U.S. is needed. Check the availability of corn at your farmers' market.

**102**

| Corn Pastry: | Filling: |
|---|---|
| 8 ears large-kerneled fresh corn, kernels removed and ground (4 cups) | 2 tablespoons olive oil |
| 1 tablespoon olive oil, heated | 1 cup, minced white onion |
| 1/4 cup evaporated milk | 1 cup peeled, minced tomato |
| 2 teaspoons sugar | 1/2 teaspoon salt, or to taste |
| 1/2 teaspoon salt | 1/4 cup raisins |
| 4 eggs | 2 hard-boiled eggs, chopped |
| | 8 green olives, pitted |
| | 1/2 teaspoon ground cinnamon |
| | 6 whole boneless, skinless chicken breasts |
| | 1 egg white |

Preheat the oven to 350°F and grease an 8-inch pan.

**For the pastry:** combine the corn and hot oil. Mix well. Add a little evaporated milk if the dough is too dry. Add the sugar, salt, and the eggs. Mix well and set aside.

**For the filling:** heat the oil in a pot over medium heat, and sauté the onion until light brown. Add the tomato and salt. Mix well and simmer for 5 minutes. Add the raisins, hard-boiled eggs, olives, cinnamon, and chicken. Mix until all ingredients are well integrated and set aside.

Pour half of the corn mixture into the prepared pan. Pour the filling on top. Pour the remaining corn mixture on top of the stuffing.

Beat the egg white and use a pastry brush to paint the top of the corn mixture.

Bake the *pastel* for 30-45 minutes, or until a knife inserted in the center comes out clean.

103

Serve the *pastel de choclo* hot.

# Roast Chicken

On Sundays when we went to the countryside for a picnic, *pollo dorado al horno* was one of the meals prepared very early in the morning to bring along. A good spot for a picnic is Mount Tunari in Cochabamba, which has a fantastic view of the valley. While the children enjoyed swimming in the icy stream of melted snow from the mountain, the adults made the salad to go with the *pollo dorado al horno*.

| | |
|---|---|
| 1 (4-pound) chicken | 1 white onion, quartered |
| 2 teaspoons salted butter | 1 lemon |
| ½ teaspoon ground black pepper | |

Preheat the oven to 350°F.

**104**

Place the chicken in a baking dish. Rub the butter and the pepper on the outside of the chicken. Place the onion inside the chicken. Squeeze the lemon into the cavity of the chicken.

Bake the chicken for 1 hour and 15 minutes. When the leg of the chicken moves easily, it is done.

Serve hot or cold with a green salad.

# Roast Turkey

The meat served by Bolivians on Christmas Eve varies from pork to turkey and duck, but *pavo al horno* is more common these days than it was when I was growing up in the 1960s because of increased U.S. influence. It is also common for some companies to give turkeys to their employees for Christmas.

| | |
|---|---|
| 1 cup butter | 16 cups cubed stale bread |
| 2 teaspoons minced garlic | 2 cups pineapple juice |
| 4 cups sliced mushroom | 1 (20-pound) turkey |
| 8 ounces slivered almonds | |

Preheat the oven to 350°F.

In a large pot over medium heat, melt the butter, and add the garlic, mushrooms, and almonds. Cook for 10 minutes. Remove from the heat and add the bread and pineapple juice. Stir to mix well. Stuff the turkey with the mixture.

**105**

Place the turkey in an oven bag, in a large roasting pan and roast for 3½–4 hours. (The bag will help the turkey to cook faster and be moist.) Use a meat thermometer to test for doneness; inserted in the thigh, it should read 185°F. An alternative is to roast the turkey at 325°F with no cooking bag. Place turkey in roasting pan and roast for approximately 5½–6 hours. The leg joint should move easily when the turkey is done.

# Roast Duck

*Pato al horno* is a special dish served on Christmas Eve and other holidays. In Bolivia, the duck used for this dish has white feathers and looks similar to a chicken. It also has white meat.

| | |
|---|---|
| 1 orange | ½ teaspoon black pepper |
| 1 (5-pound) duck | |
| 2 tablespoons salted butter | |

Preheat oven to 350°F.

Slice the orange in half and use one half for rubbing the inside of the duck and the other for rubbing the outside.

**106**

Rub the butter, salt, and pepper on the inside and outside of the duck. Tie the legs of the duck together with kitchen twine.

Place the duck in a baking dish covered with aluminum foil, and roast for approximately 15 minutes per pound. The thigh joints should move easily when done.

# Duck Stuffed with Apple

My mother used to make this dish on Christmas Eve, and my whole family loved it. The white duck meat was really tender and had a taste between turkey and chicken. Chicken can be used instead of duck, if desired. Chicken should be baked for approximately 1 hour and 15 minutes.

| | |
|---|---|
| 1 (5-pound) duck | 4 green apples, such as Granny Smith |
| 2 tablespoons salted butter | ½ cup raisins |
| ½ teaspoon ground black pepper | |

Preheat oven to 350°F.

Rub the duck with the butter, and pepper.

Peel and chop the apples, and combine with the raisins. Stuff the duck with this mixture. Place the duck in a baking dish.

107

Bake the duck for approximately 15 minutes per pound. The thigh joints should move easily when done.

# Castillian Rabbit

This recipe traditionally uses a hare, known in Bolivia as *conejo de Castilla*, or Castillian rabbit. Its meat is quite delicious.

| | |
|---|---|
| 6 tomatoes | 2 pounds rabbit, cut in 2-inch pieces |
| ½ cup olive oil | 4 cups chicken broth |
| 2 cups minced white onion | 8 medium-size potatoes, peeled and |
| 1 teaspoon minced garlic | boiled |
| 1 teaspoon salt | ¼ cup minced fresh parsley |
| ½ teaspoon ground black pepper | |

In a pot, bring water to a boil and cook the tomatoes for 5 minutes. Remove the tomatoes from the water and cool slightly. Peel, mince, and drain the tomatoes.

**108**

Heat the oil in a pot over medium heat, and sauté the onion, garlic, salt, and pepper. Add the rabbit and sauté until light brown.

Add the broth and simmer uncovered for 1½ hours until the rabbit is tender. Add more broth if necessary.

In a separate pot, boil the potatoes until tender.

Serve the rabbit with the potatoes on the side. Garnish with parsley.

# LA CARNE

In Spanish, the word for meat is *carne*, but it can also mean "flesh," depending on the context in which it is used. As a five-year-old, I have difficulty understanding the difference between "flesh" and "meat" and I think they are the same. In the midst of this confusion, I have my first questions about religion for my father.

One Friday, I attend church with my mother at Ave Maria, a small neighborhood chapel. The chapel has gothic windows and a pulpit to the right of the altar from which a Spanish priest, Father Luis, gives his sermons. They are usually long and animated. Generally, I pay more attention to his movements than to the words he says, but on that morning, my eyes wander, watching the people in the church while Father Luis is busy discussing hell and the Bible. As I am making eye contact with one of the neighbors' daughters, my mother gently pulls my ear and turns my head in the direction of Father Luis as he is saying the words *carne* and *pecado* (sin). For a moment I completely forget my mother's hand on my ear, as the word *carne* catches my total attention.

Father Luis continues in a nearly euphoric tone of voice, saying that those who succumb to the temptations of *la carne* are sinners and therefore they are destined for hell. Terrified, I look up at my mother's face and try to catch any reaction to Father Luis' words, since everyone in our family loves *la carne*. To my astonishment, my mother has no reaction at all and in fact her face seems peaceful and undisturbed by all the bad things said about *la carne*. At one point, Father Luis says that there are those who cannot have enough of *la carne* and that, with their actions, they are crucifying God on the cross. I think of myself—how much I like eating *la carne*—and I begin to worry about having anything to do with Christ's sufferings on the cross. I wish my mother hadn't heard this sermon because I think that, after this Friday service, there is not going to be any more *carne* for our family. I keep looking at Father Luis and then at my mother for any sign of a reaction from her, but find none.

After hearing Father Luis say that, as a good Christian, one should renounce the temptations and the sins of *la carne*, I pull my mother's right arm. Her head moves toward me and she quietly tells me to listen. I cannot believe my mother's indifference to all of these suggestions to eliminate *la carne* from our lives. Would she do it? For a moment I even think that she took me to church that Friday because she wants to prepare me for not having any more *carne*. I start to think fast, trying to find a solution to this plot by Father Luis to eliminate *la carne* for the good of our souls. I feel relieved that my other relatives are not there, especially Aunt Maria, since she loves *la carne*. Perhaps I could visit her more often and feast on *la carne* at her place. I am sure there has to be a way around this edict. After all, life without *la carne* doesn't seem quite right, hell or no hell.

I walk back home with my mother, and during our conversation she does not say a word about *la carne*. The first thing I do when I get home is to wait for my father, who has gone to see his brother. By this time, I suspect that we may need to change our religion, so we can continue enjoying *la carne*: I have a friend at school who once told me that his father was a Catholic before he married his mother, who converted him to being a Protestant. I decide while I wait for my father that my friend's mother may have wisely done this because she needed to have *carne* in her life. When my father comes home, I ask him who is right and who is not, when it comes to religions. My father is surprised to hear me ask this but, as he looks into my eyes, he tells me, "People like to call God by different names: some call God Christ, others Buddha, Allah, and so on. At the end, son, it is the same God." My father's answer doesn't help my problem of not eating *la carne*.

I realize that this situation is more complicated than I thought and I am beginning to make plans for the next visit to Aunt Maria's house. I wonder all afternoon why *la carne* can be such a sin when it tastes so good from my mother's kitchen. In the evening, I sit at the table resigned to give up *la carne* at home, but not at Aunt Maria's house … when the smell of *la carne* excites my senses one more time as I discover that, for dinner, we are having *carne asada al vino*, roast beef with wine sauce. Boy, am I glad my mother doesn't have the same beliefs as Father Luis.

**MY MOTHER'S BOLIVIAN KITCHEN**

# Sun-Dried Beef

**Charque**                                          **6 servings**

In Quechua, *charque* means "sun-dried beef." It is used in various Bolivian dishes.

> 2 tablespoons salt
> 2 pounds sirloin steak, thinly sliced

Sprinkle the salt over the beef, making sure there is salt on every part of it. Place in the regrigerator for 2 hours.

Wrap each slice of meat in wax paper, lay them on a tray so they do not overlap. Set the tray in the sun. You may also hang the meat on a string after wrapping it. Dry the beef for a day or two until completely dry. Dry the beef for up to 7 hours per day, but do not leave meat out overnight.

Place the *charque* in a nonreactive container in a cool, dry place. It keeps well for a few weeks.

# Carnival Stew

**Puchero de Carnaval**                                4 servings

The carnival celebration in Bolivia varies from region to region. Carnival in the state of Oruro is worth seeing, because it offers a colorful display of dances, including the *diablada* (devil's dance). During the celebration, as they dance, the dancers, who in the past were mostly miners, dance in heavy devil costumes to a church to pay tribute to the Virgin of the *Socavón* (mine). The miners believed that the devil was in the mines and this ritual dance protected them.

*Puchero* is a meal prepared for carnival, and I remember eating it in Cochabamba where carnival consisted of parades of people dressed in costumes (something like Halloween in the U.S.), playfully throwing water at each other. *Puchero* was eaten for lunch, after a long day of celebrating.

1 pound top round steak

1 cup plus 1 tablespoon minced white onion

1 carrot

½ cup dried chickpeas, soaked 10 hours or overnight

7 ounces pork sausage

2 cloves garlic, finely chopped

1 teaspoon dried oregano

1 sprig fresh mint

½ teaspoon cumin

½ pound cabbage, separated into leaves

½ cup *chuño* (page 33), soaked 10 hours or overnight

4 potatoes, peeled and halved

2 sweet potatoes, peeled and halved

1 banana squash cut into 4 pieces

4 pears

1 plantain, peeled and quartered

4 peaches, peeled

1 ear corn, husked and quartered

1¼ teaspoons salt

½ cup rice

1 tablespoon olive oil

1 teaspoon ground yellow chili

In a large pot over medium heat, combine 8 cups water, the beef, 1 cup of minced onion, and the carrot. Skim off the foam when it starts to boil. Add the chickpeas and cook for 2 hours, until the chickpeas are tender.

Add the sausage, garlic, $\frac{1}{2}$ teaspoon of the oregano, mint, and cumin, and cook for 15 minutes.

Add the cabbage and cook for 1 hour more. Add the *chuño*, potatoes, sweet potatoes, banana squash, pears, plantain, peaches, corn and 1 teaspoon of the salt, and cook until the fruit and vegetables are tender. Add additional water as needed; water must cover all the ingredients while they cook. The broth can be served as a first course before the stew.

In another pot over medium heat, bring $1\frac{1}{2}$ cups of water to a boil, then add the rice, remaining $\frac{1}{2}$ teaspoon of the oregano, and $\frac{1}{2}$ teaspoon of the salt, and reduce the heat to a simmer. Cook for 30 minutes; the rice should be mushy.

In a pan over medium heat, heat the olive oil and sauté the remaining onion until crisp. Add the yellow chili, remaining $\frac{1}{4}$ teaspoon of the salt, and $\frac{1}{4}$ cup water. Reduce the heat to low and continue cooking for 6–8 minutes. The onion mixture should be watery.

Drain the broth from the meat mixture. Cut the meat into four pieces. Place each piece in a bowl and add the fruit and vegetables from the stew. Top with the rice. Pour the sauce over the rice.

# Baked Sun-Dried Beef

*Charque Tacaska*                                                          **4 servings**

*Charque* has a unique taste. Baking gives it an extra crispness.

| | |
|---|---|
| 4 (4-ounce) pieces *charque* (page 111) | ½ teaspoon salt |
| 2 cups fava beans, peeled | ½ cup *uchu llajwa* (page 14) |
| 8 potatoes, peeled | |

Preheat the oven to 350°F. Wash the *charque* well to remove excess salt.

Place the *charque* in a pan and bake it for 15 minutes. Remove the *charque* and pound it to ⅛ inch thick, until it begins to disintegrate, then bake for an additional 5 minutes.

Cook the favas and potatoes in boiling water until tender, adding the salt 5 minutes prior to draining the water.

Serve the *charque* with 2 potatoes, ½ cup fava beans, and ⅛ cup *uchu llajwa* per person.

**114**

# Meat Patties

*Asado de Carne Molida*                                               6 servings

These are a Bolivian version of hamburgers. They are usually eaten as a snack, rather than for lunch or dinner. They are also served with regular bread, not hamburger buns.

| | |
|---|---|
| 1 pound ground sirloin | 1 egg |
| 1 tablespoon salt | 1 tablespoon chopped fresh parsley |
| 1½ teaspoons ground black pepper | 1 teaspoon olive oil |
| 2 tablespoons chopped onion | |

Combine the meat, salt, pepper, onion, egg, and parsley. Shape into a 2½-inch-thick cylinder, then wrap in wax paper and place in the freezer for one hour, until hard.

Cut the meat into 6 slices. In a pan over medium heat, heat the oil and sauté each piece until brown on both sides and cooked to the desired degree of doneness.

# Sun-Dried Beef with Rice

The yucca and the plantains in this dish are used mostly in the states of Pando, Beni, and Santa Cruz.

| | |
|---|---|
| 1 pound *charque* (page 111) | **Plaintains:** |
| 1 cup rice | 3 ripe plantains |
| ¼ cup olive oil | ¾ cup butter |
| ½ cup minced white onion | |
| ½ cup peeled minced tomato | **Yucca:** |
| 4 *achiote* seeds, soaked in 1/2 cup water | 2 medium-sized yucca, sliced into 2-inch pieces, boiled |
| ¼ teaspoon paprika | ¾ cup olive oil |
| ½ teaspoon salt | |
| 6 eggs, fried | |
| *Salsa cruda* (page 32) | |

**116**

In a pot over medium heat, bring 5 cups water to a boil and add the *charque*. Cook until tender, 10–15 minutes. Remove the *charque* from the pot, reserving the water. Pound and crumble it.

Add the rice to 2 cups of the reserved water. Simmer for 25 minutes, until tender.

Heat the oil in a pan over medium heat and sauté the *charque* until crisp. Remove the *charque* from the pan and set aside.

In the same pan, sauté the onion until light brown and crisp. Add the tomato, the strained water of the *achiote*, 1 cup water, and the salt. Cook for about 5 minutes. Stir and add the *charque*, cook for 5 minutes longer.

Stir, and add the mixture to the rice, making sure it is not too dry.

**For the plaintains:** Peel the plantains and slice them in half lengthwise. In a frying pan over medium-high heat, melt the butter and add the plantains. Cook 5 minutes on each side. Remove and drain on absorbent paper.

**For the yucca:** In a frying pan over medium-high heat, heat the oil and add the yucca. Cook 5 minutes on each side until light brown. Remove and drain on absorbent paper.

Serve the rice mixture warm, each portion topped with a fried egg and *salsa cruda*, with a slice of fried plantain and two pieces of fried yucca on the side.

# Beef with Toasted Rice

Toasted rice is used in many Bolivian dishes. Unlike steamed or boiled white rice, this type of rice does not get sticky. It is important to remember that the meat should be cooked until is very tender—to the point that it doesn't require a knife to cut it.

| | |
|---|---|
| 1 tablespoon olive oil | ½ teaspoon ground pepper |
| 1 cup rice | 1 bay leaf |
| 1 cup minced onion | 1 teaspoon minced fresh parsley |
| 2 teaspoons minced garlic | 1 pound sirloin steak, diced into |
| ½ teaspoon salt | 1-inch cubes. |

In a pot over medium heat, heat the oil and toast the rice until light brown.

**118**

Add 2 cups water and bring it to a boil, then reduce the heat to low. Add the onion, garlic, salt, pepper, bay leaf, parsley and the meat. Continue cooking until the meat is tender and the liquid is absorbed, 20–30 minutes.

# Drunken Beef

*Borracho* is the Spanish word for "drunken", and Bolivians use it to describe some dishes that include alcohol. This is ordered when Bolivians socialize, gathering for long hours with friends to play *cacho*.

| | |
|---|---|
| 2 tablespoons olive oil | 1 teaspoon ground black pepper |
| 2 cups chopped white onion | 2 tablespoons minced fresh parsley |
| 1 pound beef loin, cut into 6 pieces | 1 teaspoon dried oregano |
| 2 red bell peppers, thinly julienned | 1 cup port |
| 3 tomatoes, julienned | 2 cups light beer |
| ½ teaspoon salt | |

In a pot over medium heat, heat the oil and sauté the onion until light brown and crispy. Add the meat, and cook about 10 minutes. Add the rest of the ingredients and simmer for 3–4 hours, until the meat is tender.

**119**

**MEAT**

# Beef with Fried Eggs

*Montado* is the Spanish word for "on top," which I believe refers to the fact that the meat has fried eggs and sauce. *Lomo montado* can be found in most of the states of Bolivia.

| Beef: | Sauce: |
|---|---|
| 1 pound beef tenderloin | 2 tablespoons olive oil |
| 1¼ cups plus 1 tablespoon olive oil | 1 teaspoon garlic |
| ½ teaspoon salt | 1 cup finely diced white onion |
| 1 teaspoon ground black pepper | 1 cup chopped tomato |
| 6 medium-size potatoes, cut into 1-inch pieces | 2 tablespoons minced fresh parsley |
| Salt | ⅛ teaspoon salt |
| 6 eggs | ½ tablespoon ground black pepper |

**120**

**For the beef:** Cut the tenderloin into 1-inch thick slices, discarding the fat but leaving the silverksin that holds the meat in its natural round form.

Heat 1 tablespoon of the oil in a saucepan over medium heat, and sauté the meat until blood surfaces on the top. Add the salt and pepper. Turn over the meat and do the same thing to the other side. (Salt should be added only when the meat is nearly cooked, otherwise it will dry out.)

Put 1 cup of the olive oil in a deep pot and heat the oil until it is hot. Dry the potatoes with paper towels and place them in the pot a few at a time. Fry them until they are golden. Remove them from the pot and sprinkle with salt.

In a frying pan over medium heat, heat ¼ cup of the remaining oil and fry the eggs until the whites set. Spoon the oil in the pan over the eggs while they are cooking.

**For the sauce:** Heat the oil in a saucepan over medium heat, and sauté the onion and garlic until crisp and light brown. Add the tomato, parsley, salt, and black pepper, and cook for 10–15 minutes, stirring with a wooden spoon.

To serve, place the meat on a plate, top it with the egg and a small amount of the sauce, with the potatoes on the side. It can be served with a lettuce salad.

# Beef with *Chuño*

*Ch'ajchu* is Quechua for "splash." This meal is originally from the Altiplano region of Bolivia, but it can also be found in some of the restaurants in the valley region. As a young boy, I remember eating this meal at some of the country weddings to which my family was invited. In the 1950s, these weddings were celebrated for as long as a week and children and adults had a great time.

| | |
|---|---|
| 2 tablespoons olive oil | 4 (½-inch-thick) slices *quesillo* or feta cheese |
| ½ cup minced white onion | |
| 1 pound sirloin steak, sliced into 4 pieces | 2 hard-boiled eggs, quartered |
| ¾ teaspoon salt | *Salsa cruda* |
| 4 potatoes | ½ cup minced white onion |
| 1 cup *chuño* (page 33) | ½ cup peeled, minced tomato |
| 1 cup fava beans, peeled | 1 tablespoon minced fresh serrano chili |
| 5 green onions, chopped into 2-inch pieces | 1 tablespoom minced fresh cilantro |
| | ¼ teaspoon salt |
| 4 whole large dried red chilies | 1 teaspoon minced fresh parsley |

In a pan over medium heat, heat 1 tablespoon of the oil and sauté the onion until brown and crispy.

In a pot over medium heat, heat 4 cups water to lukewarm and add the steak with ½ teaspoon of the salt. Skim the foam and add the onion. Bring to a boil, then reduce to a simmer, and cook for 1 hour.

Add the potatoes. Return the water to a boil and add the *chuño*. Again, return the mixture to a boil and add the fava beans. Continue cooking until the potatoes are tender, 20–30 minutes. Finally, add the green onions and cook for 2–3 minutes.

Remove from the heat and drain the water, reserving 1 tablespoon. Remove the meat and pound each piece without breaking it to ¼-inch-thick. Set the meat aside in a covered pot to keep warm.

Seed the chilies and soak in warm water until soft. Drain and squeeze dry. In a mortar and pestle or food processor, process the chilies until they form a smooth paste.

In a pan over medium heat, combine the remaining 1 tablespoon of oil, chili paste, reserved cooking liquid, and ¼ teaspoon of the salt, and cook for 5–7 minutes.

**For the *salsa cruda*:** Mix the onion, tomato, and salt in a bowl.

Place all the contents of the pot in a big bowl, making sure the green onions remain on top.

Add the pounded meat. Top with the serrano chili, eggs, and cheese. Finally, add the *salsa cruda* and the parsley.

# Old Clothes

The name of this dish, *ropa vieja*, or old clothes, refers to the fact that the meat resembles tattered clothes. People eat this as an appetizer in some of the bars and restaurants in Bolivia while gathering with friends to discuss sports or politics.

| | |
|---|---|
| 1 pound sirloin steak | ½ teaspoon ground black pepper |
| 1 cup sliced white onion | 2 teaspoons white wine vinegar |
| 1 cup chopped tomato | 1 tablespoon olive oil |
| 1 minced green chili | 6 potatoes, boiled |
| ½ teaspoon salt | |

Preheat the broiler.

**124** Broil the steak to the desired degree of doneness, set aside to cool.

Slice the beef into thin, bite-size strips. Combine with the rest of the ingredients, except the potatoes and marinate for 15 minutes.

Serve with the potatoes.

# Pan-Fried Steak

In Bolivia, pan-fried steak is sometimes prepared as part of a breakfast meal—especially after an all-night party.

| | |
|---|---|
| ¼ cup olive oil | 1 tablespoon salt |
| 4 (8-ounce) sirloin steaks (see Note) | 1 tablespoon ground black pepper |

In a pan over medium heat, heat 1 tablespoon of oil until very hot and cook one slice of meat until blood surfaces on the top. Add the salt and pepper. Turn the meat over and do the same thing to the other side. (Salt should be added only when the meat is nearly cooked, otherwise it will dry out.)

Cook the meat until both sides are browned and the meat is cooked to the desired degree of doneness.

**125**

Prepare the remaining steaks as described above.

Serve immediately with potatoes, corn, and salad.

**Note:** Unless you have a big frying pan, cook the steaks one at a time.

# Spinach and Beet Stew

My mother used this stew to teach us to like spinach and beets, since my sisters and I were not too fond of them. I must say that it worked, because these days I love both vegetables.

| | |
|---|---|
| 1 pound ground beef | ½ teaspoon salt |
| 1 cup minced white onion | 4 cups shredded spinach |
| 1 cup chopped tomato | 4 cups shredded beets |
| 1 tablespoon minced garlic | 1 tablespoon olive oil |
| ½ teaspoon ground black pepper | 4 potatoes, peeled and boiled |

In a pot over medium heat, combine the meat, onion, tomato, garlic, pepper, and salt. Bring the mixture to a boil and add a little water if the mixture is too dry. When the meat is cooked, add the spinach, beets, and oil. Continue cooking for 8 minutes.

Serve with the potatoes on the side.

# Breaded Beef Cutlets

This popular meal is a favorite, eaten in the evening after going to the movies—much like people in the U.S. go out for pizza. *Sillp'anchu* is a Quechua word meaning "thin meat."

---

**Beef:**

5 (8-ounce) sirloin steaks

5 tablespoons dry bread crumbs

½ teaspoon salt

1 tablespoon ground black pepper

5 tablespoons olive oil

¾ cup olive oil

5 small potatoes, boiled and sliced

5 eggs

**Salsa:**

½ cup finely diced white onion

½ cup finely diced tomato

1 tablespoon minced fresh parsley

1 tablespoon minced fresh cilantro

½ tablespoon ground black pepper

½ tablespoon salt

1 tablespoon olive oil

---

**127**

**For the beef:** Using a flat stone or the flat side of a tenderizing mallet, pound each steak as thin as possible. As you do this, sprinkle the bread crumbs, salt, and pepper on both sides and continue pounding the meat so the crumbs stick. Each piece of meat should be the size of a dinner plate.

Heat 1 tablespoon of the oil in a large frying pan over medium heat, and sauté one steak on one side and then the other, until it is cooked through. Sauté the remaining steaks the same way, adding 1 tablespoon of oil to the pan per steak.

In the same frying pan over medium heat, heat ½ cup of the oil and fry the potatoes.

In another frying pan over medium heat, heat ¼ cup of the remaining oil and fry the eggs.

**For the salsa:** Combine all the ingredients in a bowl.

Serve the *sill'panchu* on a bed of rice. Place and egg and some salsa on top of the *sill'panchu* and the fried potatoes on the side.

# Baked Breaded Steak

The preparation of the meat for this meal is similar to *sill'panchu* (page 127) but the result is quite different. Meat lovers, like my wife Tina, are crazy about this dish. You can use regular or evaporated milk.

| | |
|---|---|
| 4 (8-ounce) sirloin steaks | 1 cup chopped tomato |
| ¾ teaspoon salt | 2 tablespoons minced fresh parsley |
| 1½ teaspoons ground black pepper | 4 small potatoes, peeled, boiled, and |
| ¼ cup dry bread crumbs | sliced |
| ½ cup plus 2 tablespoons olive oil | 2 eggs |
| 1 cup minced white onion | 1½ cups milk |

Preheat the oven to 350°F. Grease a 13 x 9-inch pan.

Season the steaks using ½ teaspoon of the salt and the pepper, and pound the meat to ¼ inch thick. As you do this, sprinkle the bread crumbs on one side of the meat, then on the other side, and continue pounding the meat so the crumbs stick.

In a pan over medium heat, heat 1 tablespoon of olive oil and fry the onion until it is golden brown and crisp. Add the tomato and parsley, then reduce the heat and simmer for 7–10 minutes.

In another pan over medium heat, heat 1 tablespoon of the olive oil and brown the meat. Do not overcook. Layer the steak in the prepared dish.

Heat the remaining ½ cup of olive oil and sauté the potatoes for 4 minutes. Then stir in the onion mixture.

Lightly beat the eggs with the milk and remaining ¼ teaspoon salt. Pour this mixture over the meat until it is completely covered.

Bake for 15 minutes, or until the egg mixture has set. This dish should be juicy, not dry.

# Fake Rabbit

**Falso Conejo**          **6 servings**

This dish is typical of the Altiplano and valley regions. *Falso conejo* means "fake rabbit." The name is a mystery to me, because the dish does not resemble rabbit in any way. So, for those who couldn't possibly make a meal from a beloved rabbit, this is a recipe to try.

| | |
|---|---|
| 6 tablespoons bread crumbs | 1 cup minced white onion |
| ½ teaspoon salt | 2 tablespoons finely chopped parsley |
| ½ teaspoon ground black pepper | 1 teaspoon minced garlic |
| 1 pound sirloin steak, thinly sliced into 6 pieces | ½ cup chopped tomato |
| 13 tablespoons olive oil | 1 cup peas |

Combine the bread crumbs, ¼ teaspoon of the salt, and pepper. Pound the meat to ⅛ inch thick. As you do this, sprinkle the bread crumbs on both sides of the meat, and continue pounding the meat so the crumbs stick.

In a deep skillet over medium heat, heat 2 tablespoons of the oil and fry each steak, 3–5 minutes on each side. Add 2 tablespoons of oil to the pan per steak. Set the steaks aside.

In the same skillet, heat the remaining 1 tablespoon of oil and sauté the onion until crisp. Add the parsley, garlic, tomato, and remaining ¼ teaspoon of the salt. Continue cooking for 5 to 10 minutes, adding water as necessary. Bring the mixture to a boil. Add the peas and cook until tender, about 10 minutes.

Finally, add the steaks and cook for 10 minutes.

Serve with potatoes, rice, or *chuño phuti* (page 34).

**MEAT**

# Stuffed Beef Rolls

It is customary for friends to gather at a bar or restaurant and play a popular game of dice, known as *cacho*. *Picana* is often ordered to accompany the gathering at the many outdoor restaurants along Prado Avenue in Cochabamba.

| | |
|---|---|
| 5 carrots, quartered | 2 cups white wine |
| 2 cups minced white onion | ½ teaspoon ground dry red chili |
| 1 cup chopped tomato | ¼ cup olive oil |
| 3 cloves garlic, minced | 1 pound top or bottom round steak, |
| ½ teaspoon cumin | cut into thin 5-inch squares |
| ½ teaspoon ground black pepper | 6 cups beef broth |
| ½ teaspoon salt | 6 potatoes, peeled and boiled |
| 1 bay leaf | 6 ears corn, boiled |
| ½ cup white wine vinegar | |

**130**

Combine all the ingredients except the beef, broth, potatoes, and corn.

Place some of this stuffing on each piece of meat and roll up the meat, placing toothpicks at each end of the roll and one in the middle, to hold the rolls shut.

Place the meat rolls and any leftover stuffing in a pot, and add the broth. Bring the broth to a boil over medium heat, then reduce the heat to low. Continue cooking for 2–3 hours, until the meat is tender.

Remove the toothpicks, and serve the meat rolls with the potatoes and corn.

# Pork Fricassee

*Fricasé* is a typical dish from La Paz but is also found in other cities in Bolivia. It is usually eaten in the late morning prior to lunch or, in some instances, at night. It is a favorite dish as part of a New Year's celebration or other party.

| | |
|---|---|
| 2 tablespoons olive oil | ½ teaspoon salt |
| ½ cup minced white onion | 2 pounds lean pork loin, cubed |
| 1 teaspoon cumin | 8 small red potatoes, peeled and |
| ½ teaspoon ground black pepper | boiled |
| 1 teaspoon dried oregano | 4 cups cooked white hominy |
| 4 teaspoons minced garlic | |

Heat the oil in a pan over medium heat, and sauté the onion until light brown and crisp. Add the cumin, pepper, oregano, garlic, and salt.

Add the pork and fry it until lightly browned.

Bring 8 cups water to a boil and reduce the heat to a simmer. Add the pork mixture. Cook the pork until it is really tender, for about 2 hours. Add more water if necessary.

Serve the *fricasé* in a soup plate, along with the potatoes and hominy.

131

# Altiplano Stew

*Picana del altiplano* is typical of the Altiplano region and similar to *picana del valle*, although it uses a variety of meats. It is a popular dish in cities like La Paz for a night out with friends playing *cacho*.

| | |
|---|---|
| 3 whole boneless, skinless chicken breasts, cut into 2-inch pieces | 1 medium tomato, peeled and thinly sliced |
| 1 pound lamb, cut into 2-inch pieces | 2 carrots, quartered |
| 1 pound lean pork loin, cut into 2-inch pieces | ½ cup minced fresh parsley |
| 1 cup peas | 2 teaspoons ground black pepper |
| 2 cups white wine | ½ teaspoon salt |
| 1 bay leaf | 2 cups beef broth |
| ¼ cup white wine vinegar | 4 ears corn, sliced into 2-inch pieces |
| 1 cup minced white onion | ½ cup flour |
| ½ cup tomato juice | 6 small potatoes, peeled and boiled |

**132**

In a pot, combine all the ingredients except the flour and potatoes.

In a bowl, mix the flour with ½ cup water to make a thin paste. Cover the pot with a piece of coarse cotton cloth, and spread the flour mixture on the cloth. Alternatively, you can use a lid set slightly askew.

Bring the *picana* to a boil, then reduce the heat to a simmer. Continue cooking for 3 hours, until the meat is tender.

Serve the *picana* in deep soup bowls with a piece of each meat, corn, potato, and plenty of broth in each bowl.

# Cracklings

The *chicharrón* cooked in the various parts of the valley in Bolivia is normally cooked in pork fat, which gives it a rich flavor. However, in the U.S. I have modified the recipe and do not use the fat. The taste is still delicious and the dish is healthier. My older sister Guichy also follows this approach in Bolivia.

| | |
|---|---|
| 3 pounds lean pork loin | ½ teaspoon salt |
| 1 teaspoon cumin | 2 tablespoon olive oil |
| 1 teaspoon minced garlic | Juice of 2 lemons |
| 1 teaspoon dried oregano | |

Wash the meat and cut it into 2-inch chunks.

In a pot over medium heat, combine the pork, cumin, garlic, oregano, salt, 1 tablespoon of the olive oil, and add enough water to cover the pork.

**133**

Bring the mixture to a boil and reduce the heat to a simmer. Stir the meat from time to time with a wooden spoon. Cook the mixture uncovered, until the meat is very tender and all the water evaporates, about 3 hours.

In a saucepan over medium heat, heat the remaining 1 tablespoon of oil and fry the pork until it is browned.

Add the lemon juice to the pork and serve with corn on the cob, a piece of feta cheese, and cucumber salad (page 24).

# Cracklings with Beer

This dish is typically made on Sundays and eaten in the afternoon at various restaurants in the city of Cochabamba or the countryside. Sometimes, my family went out to eat this dish, but other times, it was made at home with a group of curious children observing with anticipation the magic of cooking. In Bolivia, a corn drink called *chicha* is used to cook the pork. Light beer also does the job.

| | |
|---|---|
| 3 pounds lean pork loin | ½ teaspoon salt |
| 1 teaspoon cumin | 2–3 (12-ounce) cans light beer |
| 1 teaspoon minced garlic | Juice of 2 lemons |
| 1 teaspoon dried oregano | |

Wash the meat and cut it into 2-inch cubes.

**134**

Place the meat in a pot and add the cumin, garlic, oregano, salt, and enough beer to cover the meat. Leave to marinate overnight in refrigerator.

Bring the pot to a boil and reduce the heat to simmer. Continue cooking uncovered for about 1½ hours, until the pork is tender. Cook, stirring constantly until the beer evaporates. As you cook the meat, skim the foam.

Add the lemon juice to the meat and serve it with corn on the cob, a piece of feta cheese, and cucumber salad (page 24).

# *Chola* Sandwich

This is a popular sandwich sold in the streets of some Bolivian cities. The round bread used is called *tortilla*, but does not resemble Mexican tortillas. It is a 4-inch roll with cheese baked on top. The sandwich is also sold with additional ingredients such as *locoto* and *uchu llajwa*. *Locoto* is a small chili and *uchu llajwa* (page 14) is a hot sauce made with *locoto*, tomato, parsley, and onion. The following recipe has been modified slightly for those who don't like spicy foods.

| | |
|---|---|
| 4 (4-inch) pieces baguette, halved | 4 portions of *salsa cruda* (page 32) |
| 4 slices *asado de cerdo* (page 139) | |
| Pickled carrots and onions (recipe follows) | |

Place thin slices of pork on one half of the bread and add a layer of pickled carrots, pickled onions and 1 teaspoon of *salsa cruda*. Top with the other half of the bread.

**135**

# Pickled Carrots and Onions

| | |
|---|---|
| 1 cup baby carrots | ¼ teaspoon ground black pepper |
| ½ teaspoon salt | 3 cups white wine vinegar |
| 1 cup pearl onions, trimmed | |

In a pot over medium heat, boil the carrots with ¼ teaspoon of the salt in 3 cups water for 4 minutes. Drain and set aside to cool.

In a separate pot over medium heat, cook the onions with the remaining ¼ teaspoon salt for 3 minutes. Drain and set aside to cool.

Pack the carrots and onions into a glass jar. Add the pepper and vinegar to cover. Place in the refrigerator for 3 days before using.

# Rolled Pork

This dish has been one of my favorites ever since I was a kid. It was usually served after the soup at lunchtime. For years after I left home, I craved it, as I could only eat it when I went to visit my family in Bolivia. It wasn't until a year after my mother's death that I finally tried making this dish. I have modified the original recipe and omitted some of the ingredients, such as the pork skin, which I think is not really necessary. It is a good recipe to make in the summer, because it is served cold.

1 tablespoon minced garlic
1 tablespoon fresh cumin
1 tablespoon minced fresh parsley
1 tablespoon ground black pepper
1 tablespoon dried oregano
1 tablespoon minced fresh mint
⅛ teaspoon ground cinnamon
⅛ teaspoon ground cloves

1½ cups red wine vinegar
3 pounds pork loin, cut into 2-inch cubes, fat removed

Materials:
Cheesecloth
String

In a large pot, combine the garlic, cumin, parsley, pepper, oregano, mint, cinnamon, and cloves with the vinegar.

Put the pork in the pot and stir well. Marinate overnight in the refrigerator.

The next morning, pour off the marinade and place the meat on the cheesecloth. Wrap the meat as tightly as possible and then use the string to secure it. Make sure the meat is totally enclosed in the cheesecloth.

**136**

Place the wrapped meat in a vegetable steamer. Steam the meat for approximately 4 hours. You can check if the meat is fully cooked by using a wooden stick to pierce the meat. If the stick penetrates the meat easily, it is fully cooked.

Take the wrapped meat out of the steamer and immediately put something heavy on top of it to press out the water. Normally I place the meat on a cutting board and then I put another board on top. On that, I place something heavy, and leave it there for a ½ hour. Then, chill it in the refrigerator overnight.

The next day, remove the cheesecloth. Slice the meat, sprinkling it with red wine vinegar and serve with cucumber or carrot salad, and corn on the cob.

# Creole Pork Roll

This type of *enrollado* has colorful ingredients, which make it quite visually attractive and delicious.

| | |
|---|---|
| 1 recipe Rolled Pork (page 136), prepared through marination | 8 carrots, peeled and cooked |
| ½ cup peas, cooked | **Materials:** |
| 2 large beets, cooked until barely tender and peeled | Cheesecloth |
| 5 hard-boiled eggs | String |

Place the meat on the cheesecloth. Top with the peas. Place the beets directly on top of the peas. Arrange the eggs in a line end to end. Place the carrots in a line next to the eggs. This way when the *enrollado* is sliced, you'll see the yolk and white of an egg, some of the carrots, and the other vegetables.

**138**

Wrap, cook, and chill the meat according to the directions for Rolled Pork (page 136).

# Roast Pork

In Latin America there is a belief that pork is hard to digest. Therefore it is customary for Bolivians to eat pork with an alcoholic beverage, such as beer or *chicha*. As the saying goes, the alcohol serves "para matar el chancho," or "to kill the pork." In other words, the beer or *chicha* will aid digestion.

| | |
|---|---|
| 1 pound lean pork loin, cut into 3-inch chunks | 4 large dry red chilies |
| ½ teaspoon salt | 1 teaspoon minced garlic |
| 1 cup minced white onion | ¼ teaspoon paprika |
| 1 tablespoon minced fresh mint | 1 tablespoon olive oil |

In a pot over medium heat, combine the pork with enough water to cover. Add the salt, onion, and mint, and cook until the pork is tender. Drain and set aside.

139

Seed the chilies and soak in warm water until soft. Drain and squeeze dry. In a mortar and pestle or food processor, process the chilies until they form a smooth paste. In a pan over medium heat, heat ½ cup water, the garlic, paprika, and chili paste and cook for 5 minutes.

Heat the oil and sauté the pork. Add the paprika sauce.

Serve with potatoes.

# Baked Pork Leg

**Pierna de Cerdo al Horno**                                    **8 servings**

When I was a child, my mother Margarita, baked pork leg at one of our neighborhood bakeries. She thought that their oven, which used eucalyptus wood, was better for pork leg than the oven we had at home. I accompanied her to take the pork, covered with a big cotton cloth, to the bakery. We walked next to each other, my mother carrying the pork leg above my head. I was only five and I enjoyed going back and forth with her to the bakery. We went back a few hours later when it was cooked. I always got the first piece. I liked this dish so much that I always requested it for my birthdays.

This recipe tastes best when allowed to marinate for a day before cooking. The meat can also be splashed with a bottle of light beer prior to putting the ingredients in the incisions. Adding beer is not necessary, but it gives the pork a different flavor, which you may want to try sometime. The meat can also be eaten the next day as a sandwich with lettuce and tomato.

**140**

| | |
|---|---|
| 1 pork leg (about 4 pounds) | ½ cup white wine vinegar |
| Juice of 3 lemons | ½ cup minced fresh parsley |
| 1 teaspoon cumin | 1 cup peeled, chopped tomato |
| 2 teaspoons minced garlic | ½ cup minced onion |
| 3 tablespoons olive oil | ¼ cup chopped red bell pepper |
| 1 teaspoon dried oregano | 1 pound baby carrots |
| ½ teaspoon salt | |

Preheat oven to 375°F.

Remove any excess fat from the pork leg. Wash the pork leg thoroughly, then dry it with a cloth and place it in a roasting pan.

Make deep incisions with a knife all over the pork leg.

Process all the remaining ingredients, except the carrots, in a food processor or blender, until well mixed.

Place the mixture into the incisions made in the pork leg. Spread any left over mixture over the top. Insert the carrots in the incisions.

Bake the pork leg until it is completely cooked, about 2½ hours. Serve with baked potatoes, baked plantains, baked yams, and salad.

# Pork Leg with Lemon

*Pierna de Cerdo con Limón*　　　　　　　　　　　　　　**8 servings**

The lemon in this dish gives the pork a taste distinct from the other pork recipes in this book.

| | |
|---|---|
| 1 (5-pound) pork leg | 1 teaspoon dried oregano |
| Juice of 10 lemons | ½ teaspoon salt, or to taste |
| 1 cup minced white onion | 1 teaspoon ground black pepper |
| 1 teaspoon minced garlic | 1 cup white wine |
| ½ cup chopped tomato | |

Remove any excess fat from the pork leg. Wash the pork leg thoroughly. Then dry it with a cloth and place it in a large pot.

Make deep incisions with a knife all over the pork leg. Squeeze the lemon juice over the pork.

Process all the remaining ingredients except the wine in a food processor or blender until well mixed.

Stuff the mixture into the incisions.

Pour the wine into the pot and add enough water to cover the pork leg. Cook over medium heat until the pork is tender, about 3 hours.

Serve with rice and salad.

# Lamb Stew

This stew is a favorite of my sister Carla, whose voracious appetite demands more than one serving. For people who love lamb, this is a great stew to try. Lamb is eaten mostly in the valley and Altiplano regions of Bolivia.

| | |
|---|---|
| 1 tablespoon olive oil | ½ teaspoon salt |
| ½ cup minced onion | 3 pounds lamb, cubed |
| 1 tablespoon minced garlic | 6 medium-size tomatoes, peeled and |
| ½ teaspoon cumin | chopped |
| ¼ teaspoon ground black pepper | 1 cup green peas |
| 1 tablespoon dried oregano | ½ cup Spanish green olives, pitted |
| ¼ cup minced fresh parsley | |

Heat the oil in a saucepan over medium heat, and sauté the onion and garlic until light brown and crisp.

**143**

Add the cumin, pepper, oregano, parsley, and salt. Cook for 5 minutes. Add the lamb and cook until lightly browned.

Cover the pot and lower the heat to a simmer. Stir the mixture frequently so it doesn't burn. Continue cooking until the onion has completely broken down.

Add the tomatoes and cook, covered, until the meat is very tender, about 1½ hours, stirring the lamb from time to time. Add the peas and olives and cook for another ½ hour. There is no need to add water because the tomatoes will generate enough juice.

# Roast Lamb

My family often traveled to the countryside of Bolivia during Easter or sometimes in the month of June when my sisters and I had time off from school because of winter vacation. At some of the places we visited, we stayed with friends or relatives. In the 1950s, it was customary to prepare a special meal for the arriving guests. Some of these meals included *asado de cordero*, and a lamb was roast for our culinary delight.

| | |
|---|---|
| 1 leg of lamb (about 5 pounds) | ½ teaspoon ground black pepper |
| ¼ cup chili powder | 1 teaspoon dried oregano |
| 1 cup white onion, cut into 1-inch pieces | 1 teaspoon salt |
| | ½ cup white wine vinegar |
| 1 cup tomato, cut into 1-inch pieces | ¼ cup olive oil |
| ½ cup chopped fresh parsley | 6 red potatoes, peeled |
| 1 teaspoon cumin | |

**144**

Preheat oven to 350°F.

Wash the leg of lamb and dry it with paper towels. Place it in a roasting pan. Cut deep incisions on each side of the lamb.

Combine all the ingredients except the potatoes. Stuff the mixture into the incisions and pour what is left over the lamb.

Roast the lamb for ½ hour, then place the potatoes in the pan. Continue roasting for 1 hour.

# Grilled Leg of Lamb with Beer

*Asado de Pierna de Cordero a la Parrilla con Cerveza*          **8 servings**

This is the type of meal that Bolivians prepare during the weekend for friends and family.

| | |
|---|---|
| 1 leg of lamb (about 5 pounds) | Juice of 8 lemons |
| 2 (12-ounce) cans light beer | 1 tablespoon minced garlic |
| 1 cup olive oil | 1 teaspoon salt |

Cut deep incisions on each side of the lamb and place it in a deep pan. Combine the beer, oil, lemon juice, garlic, and salt and pour over the lamb. Set aside to marinate in the refrigerator for 30 minutes.

Grill the lamb over a charcoal fire or under a preheated broiler, brushing with the mixture of lemon and beer and turning occasionally until the lamb is done. Cook 20–25 minutes per pound.

Serve with salad and potatoes.

# Braised Leg of Lamb

This is a stew that is served on special occasions. It is particularly typical of the Altiplano and valley regions.

| | |
|---|---|
| 1 leg of lamb (about 2½ pounds) | 1 teaspoon ground black pepper |
| 1 tablespoon olive oil | 1 teaspoon cumin |
| 1 cup minced onion | 1 teaspoon dried oregano |
| 1 cup chopped tomato | ½ teaspoon salt |
| 1 tablespoon minced fresh parsley, plus extra for garnish | 4 cups beef broth |
| | 8 peeled potatoes |
| 2 tablespoons minced fresh mint | |

Cut the leg of lamb into 8 pieces. In a pan over medium heat, heat the oil and sauté the lamb until lightly browned.

146

Add the onion and sauté for 5 minutes. Add the tomato, parsley, mint, pepper, cumin, oregano, salt, and broth. Mix well and bring to a boil. Reduce the heat to a simmer and cook for 1 hour. Add the potatoes and cook for 20 minutes, or until tender.

Serve on a plate garnished with parsley.

# Veal Stew

This stew is cooked so that the meat is tender and easily cut with a fork.

| | |
|---|---|
| 1 tablespoon olive oil | ¼ cup minced fresh parsley |
| 1 tablespoon minced garlic | ½ teaspoon salt |
| ½ cup minced white onion | 2 pounds boneless veal, cubed |
| ½ teaspoon cumin | 6 medium-size tomatoes, peeled and |
| ¼ teaspoon ground black pepper | chopped |
| 1 tablespoon dried oregano | |

In a pan over medium heat, heat the oil and fry the onion and garlic until light brown and crisp. Add the cumin, pepper, oregano, parsley and salt. Add the veal and cook until lightly browned.

Cover, and reduce the heat to a simmer. Stir often so the stew doesn't burn. Cook for 15–20 minutes, until the onion breaks down.

147

Add the tomatoes and cook for 1½ hours or until the meat is very tender. Stir the stew from time to time. There is no need to add water because the tomatoes generate enough juice.

# Spicy Tongue

For people not accustomed to eating beef tongue, this dish may not sound appealing, but friends who try it, love it. When I lived in Puerto Rico, my friends used to drop by unannounced during lunch or dinnertime. On one occasion, a professor friend of mine, Maria Cristina, stopped by while I was having *picante de lengua* for lunch. We shared it, and she had seconds without asking the name of the dish. When I told her what the stew was made of, she couldn't believe I had fed her tongue, but she has loved the dish ever since.

| | |
|---|---|
| 4 pounds beef tongue (see Note) | 1 teaspoon dried oregano |
| 2 tablespoons olive oil | ½ teaspoon ground white pepper |
| 2 cups minced white onion | ½ cup minced fresh parsley |
| 1 tablespoon minced garlic | 1 tablespoon seeded ground red or |
| 4 medium tomatoes, chopped | yellow chili |
| 1 cup peas | 1 teaspoon salt |
| ½ teaspoon cumin | 8 small potatoes, peeled and boiled |

Cook the tongue in boiling water for approximately 2 hours, until it is soft. Remove it from the pot and let it cool. Remove the skin, which should come off easily, then slice it into ¼-inch-thick slices.

In a large pot over medium heat, heat the oil and sauté the onion and garlic until light brown and crisp. Add the tomato, peas, cumin, oregano, pepper, parsley, chili, and salt.

148

Simmer for 15–20 minutes, stirring the ingredients often so they don't burn. Add 1 cup water and cook for 30 minutes until the sauce thickens.

Add the tongue to the sauce and cook for 10–15 minutes.

This dish can be served with *chuño phuti* (page 34) if you have it, otherwise it can be served with boiled potatoes and *chuño* sauce (page 34). You can also serve it with toasted rice (page 47).

**Note:** Before you cook the tongue, hit it against something hard to make it easier to later peel off the skin.

# Tongue with Wine

This beef tongue variation has a distinctive flavor from being cooked with wine. This dish is more common in the Altiplano and valley regions of Bolivia than in the western states of Beni, Pando, and Santa Cruz.

| | |
|---|---|
| 4 pounds beef tongue (see Note) | 2 bay leaves |
| 1½ cups sliced mushrooms | 1 teaspoon ground black pepper |
| ½ cup dry white wine | 1 tablespoon minced fresh parsley |
| 2 tablespoons olive oil | 1 teaspoon salt |
| 2 cups minced onion | 1 cup peeled, thinly sliced carrots |
| 2 tablespoons minced garlic | 2 tablespoons cornstarch |
| 1 cup peeled, chopped tomato | 6 potatoes, peeled and boiled |

Cook the tongue in boiling water for approximately 2 hours, until it is soft. Remove it from the pot, reserving ½ cup of the cooking liquid, and let the tongue cool. Remove the skin, which should come off easily, then slice it ¼-inch thick.

While the tongue is cooking, marinate the mushrooms in the wine.

Heat the oil in a pan over medium heat, and sauté the onion and garlic until light brown and crisp. Add the tomato, bay leaves, pepper, parsley and salt. Cook for 15 minutes.

Drain the mushrooms, reserving the wine, and add them to the pan. Dissolve the cornstarch in the wine.

Add the tongue to the stew, along with the cornstarch mixture. Cook for 7–10 minutes.

Serve with one potato per plate.

**Note:** Before you cook the tongue, hit it against something hard to make it easier to later peel off the skin.

# Liver Stew

Liver is commonly served in the valley regions of Bolivia. For those unaccustomed to eating liver, this dish may not sound appealing at first, but it is worth trying for the tenderness of the meat and the sweetness of the onions.

| | |
|---|---|
| 2 tablespoons vegetable oil | 1 tablespoon minced fresh parsley |
| 2 cups minced onion | 1 pound beef liver, cut into 2-inch |
| 2 tablespoons minced garlic |   pieces |
| 1 bay leaf | 1 tablespoon beef broth |
| ½ teaspoon salt | ¼ cup red wine |
| ½ teaspoon ground black pepper | 6 red potatoes, peeled and boiled |

Heat the oil in a pot over medium heat, and sauté the onion, garlic, bay leaf, salt, pepper, parsley, and liver. Cook until browned, 2 minutes on each side for rare or 6 minutes for well-done.

**151**

Add the broth and wine, and bring to a boil. Remove from the heat and serve with the potatoes.

# A TRIP TO THE MOUNTAINS

Riding on my motor-cycle at 60 mph, the impact of the wind on my face makes my eyes tear. Riding with me and having the same experience, because neither of us has on glasses, is my friend Oscar. At our high school, we called him Come Gatos, Spanish for "Cat Eater." Oscar never ate cats, but he looked exactly like a character from the comic book *Condorito*. Ever since someone gave him that name, he accepted it without a problem. At times, I thought he liked the nick-name, because he even referred to himself as Come Gatos.

Early that morning, Come Gatos and I had embarked on a journey looking for treasures in the Andes Mountains. We had heard on the news about people finding ruins like Incallajta, where they discovered gold hidden by the Incas. I had also memorized some old documents my father had, in which some treasures hidden by the Incas were mentioned. In our homemade backpacks was food prepared by our mothers the night before, as well as a week's provisions, such as sardines and other canned food. Come Gatos had told his parents he was going camping with me at my family's country house in the town of Quillacollo. I had told my parents the same story except that the destination was Come Gatos' family's country house in Capinota.

My motorcycle roars like a lion at the hilly dirt roads as it climbs the challenging path. I keep shifting back and forth from low to high gear to gain momentum, and to move us toward our destination on the other side of the mountain. After hours of the roaring engine sound, we come to the top of the mountain and descend on a snakelike road. The tires make contact with the elusive dirt of the road and the low gear slows our descent. When we reach the bottom of the mountain, the road before us is as straight as an arrow. The motorcycle engine sounds a roar of release as Come Gatos and I speed like bullets into the valley guarded by giant reddish mountains.

As a sign of victory at having reached that far, and because we are excited to see the calm Lake Corani in front of us, we decide to stop and celebrate by eating the food prepared by our mothers. As if at a potluck, we each place the food containers on the ground on top of the weaving I brought to serve as our tablecloth. We begin salivating immediately, as we release the smell of food with our impatient removal of the lids. Come Gatos has *sill'panchu*, and I have *picante de pollo*. In a unison of "yum!" we dig in without exchanging a word.

After a while we discuss our plan to leave my motorcycle at the last house in the small town we arrived at that afternoon, not too far from Lake Corani. The food gives us such a burst of energy to continue our adventure that soon afterward, we pack up and continue our journey in search of treasures.

We leave my motorcycle with a peasant couple who don't speak much Spanish. We manage to communicate to the husband in Quechua that Come Gatos and I are going camping up in the mountains, and that since there are no roads where we are going, we can't get there riding my motorcycle. The man doesn't say much, but agrees to let me leave my motorcycle at his small, one-room adobe house.

Come Gatos and I wander in the mountains for days, camping without a tent and sleeping on the ground covered only with our blankets. Our roof is the sky, which at night places all the stars on its dark cloth and makes them look so bright and close that we can almost touch them, an experience that stirs us with awe. Come Gatos wakes up one night saying, "It's a little cold, isn't it?" The small eyes in his face become bigger for a second at the brightness of the night, and afterward we both start screaming, "Hello, hello, Mr. God, are you there?"

One day, our journey takes us down a deep mountain, where we set up camp instead of exploring, because darkness comes quickly. The next morning, we wake up and notice that the whole path down the mountain is man-made stairs. However, our hunger and the fact we don't have much canned food left, seems more urgent than examining the mountain with the stone stairs. We soon realize that canned food is not as good as the food prepared by our mothers. After eating our last share of sardines, we decide to go home because fatigue and insufficient food is beginning to take its toll on our stomachs and our adventurous spirit.

For two days, we walk back to my motorcycle, our stomachs complaining about the lack of food and our feet stepping slowly. Out of nowhere we hear the sound of flute and *charango*, accompanied by a drum that echoes in the mountains. Without saying a word, Come Gatos' narrow eyes stare at my face and we hear voices crying in the distance. We increase our speed as our tired legs carry us in the direction of the sound.

Suddenly, coming up the small hill in front of us, several people are dancing, singing, and crying at the same time. The man is a young Indian wearing a red and purple poncho, which creates a striking contrast to his black wool pants. He is holding a white hat in his hands, and his feet, in sandals, are stepping on the reddish soil. The face of the Indian woman dancing next to him is covered with tears. The two long black braids of her hair seem to wipe them away as she moves her head, swaying in grief. They are followed by a small, white-as-snow coffin, carried by two men. There is also a group of people who follow that farewell to life, playing the *charango* and *zampoñas*, their silent and inexpressive faces as stony as the mountains. Come Gatos looks at me again, inquiringly, and I whisper to him, "It's a funeral—the ones in front of the small coffin are the parents of the child."

Late in the afternoon, Come Gatos and I are zooming through the Andes, returning to Cochabamba with empty backpacks and no treasure, not realizing that back in the mountains—the stone-stepped peak we ignored—we had made an archaeological discovery that might have led to treasure.

As night makes its presence felt at the top of the foggy mountain range, the only treasure we dream about is the food our mothers will feed us when we reach home the next day.

A TRIP TO THE MOUNTAINS

# Christmas Turnovers with Cheese

*Pasteles Navideños con Queso* **12 Servings**

These delicious, fried cheese *pasteles* are prepared mainly during Christmastime, but can they be found all year long at some markets in the country, like in the city of Oruro where they are sold to accompany the maize drink called *api*.

| | |
|---|---|
| 5 cups flour | 1 cup evaporated milk |
| 2 teaspoons baking powder | 4 eggs, lightly beaten |
| ½ teaspoon salt | 6 cups crumbled *quesillo* or farmers cheese |
| 1 tablespoon sugar | |
| ½ cup plus 2 tablespoons vegetable oil | ½ cup powdered sugar |

In a bowl, combine the flour, baking powder, salt, sugar, and 2 tablespoons of the oil.

Combine the milk and eggs and add them to the flour mixture. Mix and knead until well combined. Cover the bowl with a cloth and set aside for 2 hours.

Roll out the dough on a lightly floured surface to a thickness of ⅛ inch. Cut the dough into circles with a 4-inch cookie cutter, or mark the dough with a 4-inch plate or bowl and cut out the imprints with a sharp knife. Pile the pastry circles on a plate and cover them with plastic wrap. Roll out the dough scraps and cut more circles. Continue rolling and cutting until all the dough is used.

Spoon 1½ to 2 generous tablespoons of cheese in the center of the circles. Dampen the edges and fold the dough over to form a half circle. Pinch and twist the edges together to seal them.

Heat the remaining ½ cup of oil in a pan over medium heat, and fry the *pasteles* until lightly browned and fragrant. Set aside to drain on paper towels. Serve hot, dusted with powdered sugar.

# Stuffed Christmas Turnovers

Here is another pastry prepared during Christmastime; these ones have meat. My aunt Lina used to make these *pasteles* and always gave them to us when we visited her during the holiday season.

| Dough: | Filling: |
|---|---|
| 5 cups flour | 1 tablespoon vegetable oil |
| 2 teaspoons baking powder | 1 cup minced white onion |
| ½ teaspoon salt | ½ pound ground sirloin |
| 1 tablespoon sugar | 2 tablespoons sugar |
| 2 tablespoons vegetable oil | ½ teaspoon salt |
| 4 eggs, lightly beaten | ½ cup raisins |
| 1 cup evaporated milk | 2 hard-boiled eggs, sliced |
| ½ cup powdered sugar | ½ teaspoon ground cinnamon |
| | |
| ½ cup vegetable oil | |

**158**

**For the dough:** In a bowl, combine the flour, baking powder, salt, sugar, and 2 tablespoons oil.

Combine the milk with the eggs and add it to the flour. Mix and knead until the mixture is well combined. Cover the bowl with a cloth and set aside for 2 hours.

**For the filling:** Heat the oil in a saucepan over medium heat, and sauté the onion until light brown and crisp. Add the meat, sugar, salt, raisins, eggs and cinnamon. Cook for about 15 minutes, then reduce heat to simmer. Continue cooking for about 15 minutes until the onions break down. Remove from the heat and set aside.

Roll out the dough on a lightly floured surface to a thickness of ¼ inch. Cut the dough into circles with a 4-inch cookie cutter, or mark the dough with a 4-inch plate or bowl and cut out the imprints with a sharp knife. Pile the pastry circles on a plate and cover them with plastic wrap. Roll out the dough scraps and cut more circles. Continue rolling and cutting until all the dough is used.

Spoon 1½ to 2 generous tablespoons of filling in the center of the pastry circles. Dampen the edges and fold the dough over to form a half circle. Pinch and twist the edges together to seal them.

Heat the vegetable oil in a pan over medium heat, and fry the *pasteles* until lightly browned and fragrant. Set aside to drain on paper towels. Serve hot, dusted with powdered sugar.

**TURNOVERS**

# Cheese, Chili, and Onion Turnovers

Whenever I break a *puka* in half, fresh from the oven with its chili pepper red-domed crust, the cheese-and-onion-scented steam escapes and I envision the Bolivia of yesteryear and a whole world of family and friends. My sister Carla and I used to ride my motorcycle seven kilometers from where we lived in the city of Cochabamba to a place where every afternoon people gathered patiently for the *pukas* to come out of the adobe oven.

**160**

**Dough:**
2 cups flour
1½ teaspoons baking powder
½ teaspoon sugar
½ teaspoon salt
¼ cup (½ stick) butter, cut into small pieces
2 egg yolks
½ cup evaporated milk or water

**Filling:**
¼ cup (½ stick) butter
1 cup minced onion
2 cups (about ¾ pound) crumbled *quesillo* or feta cheese

1 small hot fresh chili, such as jalapeño, seeded and minced (optional)
2 scallions, minced
2 tablespoons minced peeled tomato
4 teaspoons minced fresh parsley
2 tablespoons mild ground dried red chili
12 large black olives, pitted and halved

**Glaze:**
1 tablespoon mild ground dried red chili
1 tablespoon butter

**For the dough:** Thoroughly mix together the dry ingredients in a mixing bowl.

Cut the butter into the flour mixture with two knives, a pastry blender, or your fingertips, until it resembles coarse meal. Blend in the egg yolks and then the evaporated milk. Gather the dough into a ball. Add more milk or water, ½ teaspoon at a time, if the dough is too dry. Do not knead the dough, or it will become tough. Wrap the dough in a cloth and set aside for 2–3 hours.

Preheat the oven to 400°F and grease 2 baking sheets.

**For the filling:** Melt the butter in a large skillet over medium heat. Sauté the onions, stirring occasionally, until soft, about 10 minutes. Stir in the cheese, fresh chili, scallions, tomato, parsley, and ground chili.

**For the glaze:** Combine the ground dried red chili, butter, and 1 tablespoon water in a small saucepan. Cook the glaze over low heat for 5 minutes, and then remove it from the heat.

Roll out the dough on a lightly floured surface to a thickness of ⅛ inch. Cut the dough into circles with a 3-inch cookie cutter, or mark the dough with a 3-inch plate or bowl and cut out the imprints with a sharp knife. Pile the pastry circles on a plate and cover them with a cloth. Roll out the dough scraps and cut more circles. Continue rolling and cutting until all the dough is used.

Spoon 1½ to 2 generous tablespoons of the filling in the center of each pastry circle. Press 2 olive halves into the filling. Lay another pastry circle on top. Moisten the edges and seal the circles by pressing down on the edges first with your fingertips and then with the tines of a fork. (If the *pukas* are not sealed completely, a little bit of the filling will ooze out during baking.)

Arrange the turnovers on the prepared baking sheets and brush the tops with the glaze. Bake the *pukas* on the upper rack of the oven until the edges are golden brown, about 12 minutes. Transfer the *pukas* to wire racks and serve warm.

# Meat Pies

This crusty golden snack can be made with chicken or beef. It is eaten at parties, birthdays, or at *salteñadas*, parties where the main appetizer is a *salteña*.

---

**Filling:**
1 cup olive oil
½ cup chili powder
¼ teaspoon cumin
¼ teaspoon ground black pepper
¼ teaspoon dried oregano
½ teaspoon salt
1 cup minced white onion
1 tablespoon sugar
1 teaspoon white wine vinegar
1 tablespoon minced fresh parsley
½ cup peeled, diced, cooked potatoes
¼ cup cooked peas
1½ tablespoons unflavored gelatin
2½ cups diced sirloin steak, trimmed
24 black olives, pitted and halved
½ cup seedless raisins
6 hard-boiled eggs, sliced

**Dough:**
6 cups flour
¾ cup vegetable oil, heated
6 eggs
¼ cup sugar, or to taste
1 cup warm water
1 teaspoon salt

**Glaze:**
3 tablespoons olive oil
½ teaspoon seedless ground red chili
¼ teaspoon salt

---

162

Preheat the oven to 350°F and grease 2 baking sheets.

**For the filling:** Heat the oil and chili powder in a saucepan over medium heat. Cook for 6 minutes, then add the cumin, pepper, oregano and salt. Simmer, stirring for 8 minutes.

Add the onion and cook for 8 minutes. Remove from the heat and add the sugar, vinegar, parsley, potatoes, and peas.

Heat the gelatin and 1½ cups water in a pot over medium heat, and bring to a boil. Add the meat, then remove from the heat. Combine the meat mixture with the potato mixture and add the olives, raisins and eggs. Chill in the refrigerator overnight.

**For the dough:** combine the flour and hot oil with a wooden spoon. Set aside to rest for 7 minutes.

Add the eggs, sugar, warm water and salt and mix and knead until the mixture is well combined.

Transfer the mixture to a floured surface and knead. Cover the dough with a cloth and set aside for 15 minutes.

Divide the dough into golf ball-size pieces. Use a rolling pin, form each ball into a circle, ⅛ inch thick and 7 inches in diameter.

Spoon 1½ to 2 generous tablespoons of filling in the center of each circle. Dip your finger in water and run it around the edge of the dough. Fold the dough over to form a half circle. Seal the dough by pinching and twisting the edge. Assemble the rest of the *salteñas* in the same way.

**For the glaze:** whisk together the oil, chili, salt, and 2 tablespoons of water.

Arrange the filled *salteñas* on the prepared baking sheets and brush the tops with the glaze. Bake the *salteñas* on the upper rack until the edges are golden brown, about 8 to 10 minutes. Serve warm.

# Cochabamba Empanadas

This type of empanada is usually eaten in the afternoon at teatime. People also eat them with soda at bakeries where they are made every day. It is common to bring these empanadas home for an afternoon of socializing with friends and family. They are often accompanied by teas, such as cinnamon or *trimate*.

| | |
|---|---|
| 3 teaspoons baking powder | 3 egg yolks |
| 1 teaspoon sugar | 4 cups flour |
| 1 teaspoon salt | 2½ cups *quesillo* or *queso fresco* |
| ½ cup shortening, melted | |
| 1 cup evaporated milk or warm water | |

**164**

Mix the baking powder with the sugar, salt, shortening, and milk.

Add the eggs and the flour, little by little, until you have a dough that is not too dry. Mix the dough until you get all the air out of it.

After this, put the dough in a container, brush with oil, and let the dough rise for 30 minutes.

Preheat the oven to 350°F and grease 2 baking sheets.

Divide the dough into quarters and each quarter into 10 pieces. With a rolling pin, roll each piece into a 3-inch circle. The dough should not be too thin. Add 2 tablespoons of cheese to the middle of each circle. Add another circle of dough on top. Moisten the edges and seal the circles by pinching and twisting them together so that the cheese won't come out when the empanadas bake. You can also press the tines of a fork around the edges.

Bake the empanadas for 20 minutes.

# TODOS SANTOS

November 1 is the Day of Todos Santos (All Saints) in Bolivia, and people who have lost loved ones gather on the day before for a bread-baking ritual—the warm, crusty cheese-filled empanada or the tawny wheat bread with its golden cheese topping that looks as if it came out of a biblical movie I saw as a child. Or the *bizcocho* whose golden warmth is capable of tempting anyone. The steamy aroma of these breads reaches every corner of Cochabamba and even seems to reach heaven—perhaps searching for the souls of parents, sisters, brothers, and friends—as the chorus of baking continues in every house in town. On October 31, it is customary for children to go out at night, like children do on Halloween in the U.S., visiting from house to house and praying for the departed. In return, they get homemade bread or cookies.

Bread for this celebration comes in many shapes—animals, dolls, and other toys. Each house has an altar covered with bread and cookies, flowers, and candles. The relatives of the deceased sat in the living room while my cousin Gener and I prayed for the souls of their loved ones. I glanced at these family members and saw their lips moving, praying along with us. The long white candles on the altars crackled from time to time while they burned, and this distracted me from praying. Gener told me that the sound indicated the presence of the souls we prayed for. I wondered if those souls were tempted to eat the bread as much as I was, but never mentioned this to my cousin because I was afraid he might respond with a story I didn't want to hear.

Gener, a teenager eleven years my senior, had his own cotton bag much bigger than mine, because he could carry a heavy load of bread on his back. He was a champion at praying quickly, and he even knew how to sing some of the prayers. He always ended up with so much bread that I thought he could easily open a bakery. My mother let me go with him because he was older and could take care of me, which he did. My cousin and I always returned with enough bread and cookies to last the whole week. His mother, my Aunt Maria, even made bread soup with some of his loot.

On the Day of the Dead, praying took place at the Cochabamba cemetery, a unique experience. It became quite crowded outside the cemetery, where people laid their bread and cookies on colorful wool weavings. This cultural tradition was like a huge farmers' market, with only baked goods. There were also street vendors selling refreshments, as at any other type of public activity.

When I was five I joined that mass of people, holding my mother's hand as we walked to the cemetery, along with my sister, Guichy. I was wearing shorts with suspenders and a white T-shirt that matched my white socks. Before we reached the gate, my mother ran into an old friend of hers. I heard her say, "Gaby, it's great to see you. Are you here to visit your mother's grave?"

An attractive woman in her thirties, with curly hair and a round face, looked down at me and said, "Hi, young man!"

I looked up at her and, from my height, noticed how her green cotton dress was covering her rounded hips. I said to myself that she was a good-looking lady. I smiled at her, saying "Hi!" with a sigh as I let my small, sweaty hand slip from my mother's grasp.

I began looking around the busy surroundings until my eyes were attracted by a piece of bread in the shape of a horse, a few steps from us. Next to the small altar of bread there was a woman having prayers said in memory of her dead husband. A man approached her and started praying, and I could hear his murmuring words in my ears. The murmuring seemed to come from all over, this praying for the souls of the dead. There were other people with more altars of bread all around. It was as if the people were the instruments of those voices praying with no end on that busy afternoon. I walked on, looking at the shapes of the bread and smelling its presence. Without realizing it, I got lost in this theater of prayer.

When I decided to go back to my mother talking to the lady named Gaby, I saw a piece of bread shaped like an airplane. I asked the two women who had this altar of bread how many prayers I would have to say to get the bread plane. Their answer was three Holy Fathers and three Holy Mothers. Without hesitation, I knelt on my bare knees to pray. Holding my hands together, I prayed as fast as I could, thinking about how my cousin Gener did it. After I completed my prayers they gave me the airplane. As the hand of the woman who gave it to me lifted it off the altar, I imagined it was flying toward me.

I held the plane in my hands, and it smelled good. I resumed looking for my mother and sister, but the altars all looked the same and the praying voices repeated and repeated with no end, like the human maze I was in. I walked in all directions as fast as I could, pushing the people in front of me aside. I realized I was lost in that ocean of people. I began calling my mother as loudly as I could and kept walking, looking for any sign of them or the lady with the green dress. I walked and walked and lost all notion of time. All I knew was that it was getting late and that people were staring at me, because I was calling for my mother. I could hardly see them, because by this time the tears in my eyes had blurred their images.

A voice from nowhere said, "Have you lost your mom, child?" My left hand squeezed the airplane while I wiped the tears with my right hand so I could see where the voice was coming from. It belonged to a woman with freckles on her face and brown hair on top of her head in braids. She wore a white apron tight around her waist, which made the protuberance of her stomach even bigger. She looked pregnant and had a motherly attitude in the way she spoke to me. I stopped crying and noticed that she was selling peanut and peach drinks from a table full of glasses covered with small tin dishes. There were bees flying above the table, desirous of the sugar in the drinks.

The woman told me in a reassuring tone of voice, "Wait here for your mother, she will find you!" Then she answered one of her customers, who pointed to one of the covered glasses holding a peanut drink. In my mind I tasted the rich, milky peanut drink, but suddenly I felt a deep sadness as two warm, salty tears reached my mouth. While I sat next to the woman's table, thoughts that I would never again see my mother came to my mind, and my heart sighed and ached in desperation.

When I think about my mother these days, sometimes I feel lost because I am amidst life and she is no longer here. I look back and see myself sitting next to the woman, the strong scent of cinnamon emanating from her peanut drinks. Along her table, the voices of people move with the wind through the cemetery. Amid this world of confusion, I suddenly find my mother's eyes and see her running toward me, followed by my sister. My mother's arms raise to clasp me close while the tears on her face are stolen by the dusty wind of the afternoon.

**TODOS SANTOS**

# Tortilla Bread

In Bolivia, *tortilla* is a kind of bread with a cheese topping. It is eaten daily at breakfast and lunch.

| | |
|---|---|
| 1½ teaspoons baking powder | 1 egg |
| 1½ teaspoons sugar | 2½ cups flour |
| ½ teaspoon salt | 2 cups crumbled *quesillo* or farmers' cheese |
| 1 cup vegetable oil, warmed | |
| ½ cup evaporated milk or warm water | |

Preheat the oven to 350°F. Grease a baking sheet.

Combine the baking powder, sugar, salt, ½ cup of the warm oil, and the evaporated milk.

Beat in the egg and the flour, little by little, until you have a dough that is not too dry. Mix the dough until you have pressed the air out of it.

Put the dough in a container, lightly oil the top of it, and allow to rest for five minutes.

On a lightly floured surface, roll out the dough into ½-inch thick, 3-inch diameter pieces. Avoiding the edges of the dough, brush the top of each piece with some of the remaining oil, scatter ⅓ cup of cheese on top, and then drizzle with more oil. (Adding the oil will prevent the cheese from burning while baking.)

Place the bread on the prepared pan and bake for 30–45 minutes.

# All Saints' Sweet Bread

*Bizcocho de Todos Santos*                                    **60 pieces**

This soft sweet and delicious bread is traditionally made for All Saints Day on November 1. My mother used to make this recipe in memory of deceased relatives. Currently, my sister Mary continues the tradition by baking this bread for All Saints' Day, to honor the memory of our parents. She is the one who sent me the recipe for this book.

| | |
|---|---|
| 1 cup warm water | 15 eggs, separated plus 2 whole eggs |
| 1 teaspoon baking powder | 1 tablespoon ground cinnamon |
| 2¼ cups sugar | ½ cup Pisco or orange liqueur |
| 12 cups flour | 1¼ cups shortening |

Combine the warm water, baking powder, ½ cup of the sugar, and 1 cup of the flour in a medium-size bowl. Set aside for 10 minutes.

**170**

In a very large bowl, beat the egg whites until stiff peaks form. Slowly add the remaining 1¾ cups of sugar, beating until incorporated. Add the yolks, cinnamon, and Pisco, and beat for 5 minutes. Slowly add the baking powder mixture and then the remaining 11 cups of flour until a soft dough forms. Mix in the shortening.

Remove the dough from the bowl and grease the bowl. Return the dough to the bowl and set aside to rise for 2 hours.

Preheat the oven to 350°F and grease 6 baking sheets.

Oil your hands and divide the dough into pieces the size of tennis balls. Flatten each ball of dough slightly so it can be folded in half. Shape each ball into an oval. On the opposite side from the fold, make 2 (1-inch) incisions, cutting all the way through the dough. Arrange the bizcochos on the prepared baking sheets. Set aside for 10 minutes prior to baking.

In a small bowl, beat the remaining 2 eggs. Brush the beaten eggs over the bizcochos. Bake on the upper rack of the oven until the edges are golden brown, about 10 minutes. A knife inserted in the center will come out clean. Serve warm with tea. ✳ really bake 25 – 45 mins

# Bolivian Carrot Cake

*Pastel de Zanahoria*        **4 servings**

This pastry is ideal for an afternoon tea with friends.

| | |
|---|---|
| 2 cups peeled, grated carrots, steamed | 1 teaspoon baking powder |
| 3 eggs, lightly beaten | ½ teaspoon salt |
| ½ cup evaporated milk | 2 tablespoons vegetable oil |
| ½ cup flour | 2 tablespoons sugar |
| | 2 tablespoons dry, shredded *quesillo* |

Preheat the oven to 350°F. Grease an 8-inch square pan.

In a bowl, combine the carrots, eggs, milk, flour, baking powder, and salt. Whisk the mixture until smooth. Add the oil, sugar, and cheese, and mix well.

171

Pour the mixture into the prepared pan and bake for 20 minutes, or until a knife inserted in the center comes out clean.

# Cinnamon Rolls

This is another type of sweet bread that can be used for teatime.

| | |
|---|---|
| 2 tablespoons baking powder | 2½ cups flour |
| 6 tablespoons sugar | 2 teaspoons ground cinnamon |
| 2 teaspoons salt | 2 tablespoons honey |
| ½ cup vegetable oil, warmed, plus extra oil | ¼ cup walnuts, chopped |
| | ¼ cup raisins |
| 2 cups evaporated milk or warm water | ¼ cup butter |
| | 1 egg yolk |
| 3 eggs | |

In a large bowl, mix the baking powder with 2 tablespoons of the sugar, the salt, warm oil, and evaporated milk.

Add the eggs and the flour, little by little, until you have a dough that is not too dry. Mix the dough until you have pressed all the air out of it.

Put the dough into a container, lightly oil the top of it, and allow the dough to rise for 45 minutes.

Preheat the oven to 350°F and grease an 8-inch square pan.

Roll out the dough on a lightly floured surface, to a square form with a thickness of ½ inch. Sprinkle the cinnamon over the surface. Sprinkle with the honey and the remaining 4 tablespoons of sugar, then sprinkle with the walnuts and raisins. Dot evenly with the butter.

Roll up the dough carefully and cut into 2-inch slices. Pinch 1 end of each slice shut. Assemble the rest of the cinnamon rolls in the same way and place, closed end down, in the prepared pan.

In a bowl, combine the egg yolk and 1 tablespoon water, and apply with a pastry brush to the surface of the cinnamon rolls.

Bake for 30 minutes.

# Christmas Doughnuts

*Buñuelos de Navidad*     **12 servings**

Usually served with breakfast, these doughnuts are customarily made during Christmastime.

| | |
|---|---|
| 2 cups warm water | 4 eggs |
| 2 tablespoons sugar | 4 cups flour |
| 2 tablespoons baking powder | 1 cup vegetable oil |
| ½ teaspoon salt | 1 cup powdered sugar or molasses |

In a bowl, mix ½ cup of the warm water and the sugar until the sugar is dissolved. Add the baking powder and set aside for 6 minutes. Add the remaining water, the salt, and eggs, stirring constantly.

Slowly add the flour, a little at a time and stir into a watery mixture. Set aside until the mixture has doubled in size, about 30 minutes. The dough is ready when it sinks in the center.

**173**

With teaspoon-size pieces of dough, form doughnut shapes. With wet fingers, stretch the dough into a circular form with a hole in the center.

In a pan over medium heat, heat the oil to 350°F. Fry and turn the *buñuelos* until golden brown on both sides.

Set on paper towels to drain. Serve hot with powdered sugar or molasses on top.

# Condensed Milk Cake

*Queque con Leche Condensada*                                    **6 servings**

My cousin Beatriz, who lived in the state of Oruro used to make this cake for teatime. Its rich sweet taste of condensed milk mixed with orange liqueur is quite inviting.

| | |
|---|---|
| 2 (14-ounce) cans condensed milk | 2 tablespoons butter, melted |
| 1 cup flour | 1 tablespoon orange liqueur |
| ½ cup sugar | 1½ cups evaporated milk |
| ½ teaspoon baking soda | 1 cup shredded fresh or dry coconut |
| 3 eggs, lightly beaten |    or flaked unsweetened coconut |

Preheat the oven to 350°F. Grease 5 baking sheets.

Bring 6 cups water to a boil in a pot over medium heat. Remove from the heat and immerse the unopened cans of condensed milk in the water and leave them there for 5 minutes.

In a bowl, combine the flour, sugar, and baking soda. Add the eggs, butter, and orange liqueur. Mix thoroughly. Slowly add the evaporated milk, a little at a time. Mix until soft and smooth. Divide the mixture into nine pieces. Use a rolling pin to flatten the dough into circles ⅓ inch thick and 10 inches in diameter. Prick the dough with a fork.

Place 2 pieces of dough on each baking sheet and bake for 20–30 minutes, until golden brown. Remove from the oven. Spread the condensed milk and coconut evenly on each piece.

Stack the pieces on top of each other.

# Nut Cake

*Queque de Nuez*           **8 servings**

My high school friend Eddy and I used to buy this cake at some of the cafes in our home town of Cochabamba.

| | |
|---|---|
| 3 cups flour | 1 cup ground walnuts |
| 3 teaspoons baking powder | ¾ cup sugar |
| 5 eggs, separated | 1 cup milk |
| ⅓ cup butter, melted | ⅛ teaspoon salt |

Preheat the oven to 350°F. Grease the bottom of an 8-inch square pan.

Combine the flour and baking powder. Set aside.

In a medium-size bowl, beat the egg whites until soft peaks form.

Add the egg yolks one at a time, then the butter, walnuts, sugar, milk, salt, and the flour mixture. Mix thoroughly.

Pour the mixture into the prepared pan and bake for 20–30 minutes, or until a knife inserted in the center comes out clean.

# Papaya Cake

Queque de Papaya                                                            **6 servings**

The soft and tasty papaya flavor of this cake makes it good for breakfast or teatime.

| | |
|---|---|
| 1 egg | ½ cup walnuts |
| 1 cup sugar | ¼ teaspoon ground nutmeg |
| ½ cup butter, melted | ½ teaspoon ground cinnamon |
| 1 cup peeled, seeded, and diced papaya | ¼ teaspoon powdered ginger |
| | 1¼ teaspoons baking powder |
| 3 tablespoons cold water | 2 teaspoons lemon juice |
| 2½ cups flour | 1 cup raisins |

Preheat the oven to 350°F. Grease the bottom of a 13 x 9-inch pan.

In a food processor, process the egg, sugar, butter, papaya, and cold water.

In a bowl, combine the flour, walnuts, nutmeg, cinnamon, ginger, baking powder, lemon juice, and raisins. Slowly add the egg mixture, a little at a time, and mix until well combined.

Put the dough in the prepared pan and bake on the upper rack of the oven for about 50 minutes, until the cake turns a dark color or a knife inserted in the center comes out clean.

MY MOTHER'S BOLIVIAN KITCHEN

# Sponge Cake

This soft moist cake flavored with cognac is a good choice after dinner or for teatime.

| | |
|---|---|
| 2 cups flour | 1½ cups sugar |
| 2 teaspoons baking powder | 1 teaspoon lemon juice |
| 10 eggs | 1 teaspoon cognac |

Preheat the oven to 350°F. Grease the bottom of a 13 x 9-inch pan.

Combine the flour and baking powder. Set aside.

In a medium-size bowl, beat the egg whites until soft peaks form.

Add the sugar. Then add the egg yolks one at a time. Add the lemon juice, and then, the flour mixture. Mix thoroughly. Stir in the cognac.

Pour the mixture in the prepared pan and bake for 20–30 minutes, or until a knife inserted in the center comes out clean.

# Holy Week Sweet Bread

**Bizcocho de Semana Santa**  **12 Servings**

This sweet bread, usually prepared during Holy Week, is great served with tea or eaten alone as a snack.

| | |
|---|---|
| **Cake:** | ½ teaspoon salt |
| 4½ cups flour | 1 teaspoon lemon juice |
| 1½ cups evaporated milk, warmed | |
| ½ cup plus 2 tablespoons sugar | **Topping:** |
| 3 tablespoons baking powder | 1 egg white |
| 2 egg yolks, lightly beaten | ½ cup sugar |
| ½ cup vegetable oil, warmed, plus 1 teaspoon | |

Preheat the oven to 350°F. Grease a baking sheet.

Toast the flour in a low oven for 4 minutes, until warm.

In a bowl, combine ¼ cup of the warm milk, 2 tablespoons of the sugar, and the baking powder. Set aside for 7 minutes.

Make a well in the warm flour, then add the milk mixture to the pan. Do not mix; let it rise for 5 minutes.

Add half the beaten egg yolks, beating constantly, then beat in the remaining egg yolks. Continue beating. Slowly add the warm oil a little at a time, then add ½ cup of sugar, the salt, lemon juice, and the remaining 1¼ cup warm milk. Mix and knead until the mixture is well combined. The mixture should feel wet not dry.

Place the mixture into a greased bowl. Spread 1 teaspoon of oil on top of the mixture. Cover the pan with a cloth and let rise for 30 minutes.

Roll out the dough on a lightly floured surface to a thickness of ½ inch. Cut the dough into circles with a 3-inch cookie cutter. Pull each piece of dough into an oval shape. Make 1-inch incisions along one side of the dough. Let it rise again for 45 minutes.

**For the topping:** Beat the egg white with 1 teaspoon of water. Brush this mixture on the *bizcochos,* and sprinkle with the sugar.

Place the *bizcochos* on the prepared pan, 1 inch apart, and bake for 25 minutes, until golden.

# DOMINGO

When I was growing up, eating involved sitting at the table with my family. At each meal, we created memories like the frames in a film. My mother's kitchen fed everyone from family and friends, to the poor and also animals. The cats in my parents' house ate the same soup we had for lunch. The cats had a place in one corner of the kitchen, where one of their dishes—made of sardine cans—held the soup of the day with pieces of meat in it. My mother fed our cats not only her soups, which they enjoyed, but a healthy diet of salads and fruit as well, though

not all the cats were salad lovers, and some simply had peculiar preferences. Pinocchio, my sister Carla's cat, loved cucumber salad and also waited, alert and patient, while my mother peeled his favorite fruit, papaya.

During the eighteen years that I lived with my family, I saw many cats enjoy and benefit from my mother's cooking. Two cats, Domingo and Tongo, come to mind from time to time. Domingo was a handsome black cat with striking green eyes, who showed up one day in my mother's kitchen and never left … well, except once, but I will tell you about that later. My three sisters and I had no problem adding this cat to the family. Even my father seemed to agree, though he didn't say a word. Perhaps he felt there were too many of us for him to disapprove of Domingo's arrival.

The cat arrived on a Sunday morning when my mother was preparing lunch; that is how she named him Domingo, Spanish for Sunday. Domingo spent most days keeping her company in the kitchen. One peculiar thing about him was that he seemed genuinely interested in what my mother said, since she liked talking to him as if he were a person. The one-way conversation was sometimes about my mother's thoughts, or stories she used to tell. Domingo would stare at her while she spoke. I used to sit on a small wooden chair in the kitchen and, with my hands on my chin, listen to my mother's gentle voice addressing Domingo and me.

One of those days, when the time came to cut the meat for dinner, I heard my mother say to Domingo, "I don't like cats who steal meat; it is not good. It is better to ask for it, but never take any meat from the table."

I believe Domingo understood the rules made by my mother, because he never stole any meat as some other cats did, including Pinocchio. He was a real thief. Pinocchio stole meat from the kitchen when my mother wasn't looking, or sometimes he even stole it from a plate right on the table. Once, my father was eating a piece of *sill'panchu* and Pinocchio came to him, purring and sitting on my father's lap. Before he realized it, the meat on his plate was gone. So was Pinocchio, who usually disappeared until the next day, when he did those things. I guess he waited for things to cool off and perhaps believed we would forget about it.

By contrast, Domingo could be left in the kitchen with a piece of meat in front of him and he never would touch it unless it was given to him. He wouldn't even sniff it. What willpower he had! One day, a year after Domingo's arrival at our home, he carried a little black kitten in his mouth and carefully placed it on the kitchen floor. That afternoon, as I came into the kitchen, I heard my mother asking Domingo questions. "Is this your son?" she asked, after lifting the small animal in her hands and looking to see if it was male or female.

The kitten lay on her hands upside down, moving its paws while its head looked down to the floor. Domingo sat on the floor, his long black tail moving left and right. He looked to my mother as if for approval.

"He wants his son to live with us, Mom!" I said, hoping my mother would give in and accept Domingo's son. I asked my mother, "What is his name going to be?" The answer came after a moment of silence. With a subtle smile on her face, she said, "Tongo, his name will be Tongo."

I never knew if Tongo was a rebel or simply didn't like to follow my mother's instructions, or perhaps he thought himself some kind of hunter. My sisters and I took care of Tongo, but one day he did something that was not approved of in my mother's kitchen. He stole a big piece of meat

182

from the table as my mother was getting ready to cut it. Tongo was still young; he was too small to carry it away. He ended up with the piece of meat under the table. My mother was very upset. What she was about to cook for dinner lay on the floor with Tongo's toothmarks. I told my sister Carla that she could have my share of meat for dinner that day, but somehow she didn't seem to appreciate my gesture.

Minutes later, my mother slapped Tongo and boxed his ears, saying, "Thief, I don't want you here in my kitchen!" During this commotion, Carla and I woke Domingo from his catnap and placed him on the ground next to his son. We thought perhaps he could give his son a cat spanking, but he just sat there as if he were listening to my mother's words.

My mother looked at Domingo and told him, "Take your thief son away from my kitchen and leave him where you took him from. I don't want him in this kitchen or this house any longer."

That day the dinner menu was changed to a vegetarian meal. Our meat was bought fresh every day from the market and by that hour it was too late to replace it.

The next morning, Carla's words brought my mother to the patio, as she looked in the direction of the roof, "He is going away, he is going away. Domingo is taking his son away!" That early morning, my sleepy eyes saw Domingo on the roof with Tongo in his mouth. Domingo was carrying him across the roof. Tongo's legs and tail bumped along the roof tiles; his closed eyes showed a sign of resignation as Domingo took him away.

My mother stood there unable to react to Domingo's behavior until suddenly I heard her saying, "Come back, Domingo, bring your son back!" Domingo didn't react to my mother's pleading words, just continued slowly walking on his decisive journey over the roof. I looked at my mother's face and it had a shadow of sadness like a cloud moving. Then a sound came from her heart: "He is gone!" The three of us looked at the roof and started a unison choir that remained unanswered that day: "Domingo! Domingo! Domingo!"

Domingo came back the next day and he sat in the small chair my mother had in her kitchen. My mother implored Domingo to bring his son back. I always thought the conversations she had with animals were one-way, but when I saw Domingo bring back his son Tongo in his mouth the same way he did the first time, I thought perhaps those conversations weren't that one-sided after all. Domingo and Tongo became part of our lives and family as beloved pets. Years later when Domingo departed from life, there wasn't any word my mother could say to keep him alive. The sadness we experienced from his death was repeated years later when death claimed Tongo. We buried him in our garden in a shoe-box coffin next to his father. Their lives placed seeds of memories in our hearts. From time to time, I think about our pets and my mind holds as tightly to these memories as the claws of Domingo and Tongo held onto my clothes.

# Cherimoya Ice Cream

The rich, sweet taste of cherimoya makes this ice cream an exotic dessert to try. You can find this Andean fruit in some supermarkets.

| | |
|---|---|
| 1 (12-ounce) can evaporated milk | 1 cup seeded cherimoya puree |
| 1 cup sugar | |

Chill the evaporated milk in the refrigerator for at least 3 hours, or overnight.

In a bowl, beat the evaporated milk until smooth and tripled in volume. Add the sugar slowly while continuing to beat.

Add the cherimoya and mix well.

Pour the mixture into an ice cream maker and process according to the manufacturer's instructions.

# Cinnamon Sorbet

Cinnamon gives this sorbet a pink color. It has an icy sweet taste that resembles a snow cone. In the valley region, cinnamon sorbet is served with *chicha* and strawberries in a creation called *garapiña*.

| | |
|---|---|
| 3 cinnamon sticks | 2 tablespoons cornstarch |
| 1 cup sugar | 1 tablespoon lemon juice |
| 2 tablespoons ice water | |

Bring 5 cups water to a boil in a pot over medium heat. Add the cinnamon sticks and sugar. Cook until the water has acquired a reddish color from the cinnamon, about 40 minutes.

In a small bowl, combine the ice water and the cornstarch, and add the lemon juice. Add this mixture to the cinnamon water. Cook for 5 minutes. Remove from heat and let cool to lukewarm.

Pour the mixture into an ice cream maker and process according to the manufacturer's instructions.

# Milk Ice Cream

*Helado de Leche*                                                    **6 servings**

Cinnamon gives this ice cream a delicious flavor and makes this a good dessert to try.

| | |
|---|---|
| 4 cups evaporated milk | 1 cinnamon stick |
| 1 egg yolk, lightly beaten | 1 cup sugar |

In a pot over medium heat, combine the evaporated milk, egg yolk, cinnamon stick, and sugar. Cook until the mixture is reduced to a thick, syrupy consistency, about 8 minutes.

Remove from the heat and let cool to lukewarm.

Pour the mixture into an ice cream maker and process according to the manufacturer's instructions.

**187**

# Milk Ice Cream with Lemon

*Helado de Leche con Limón* 4 servings

The lemon flavor of this dessert leaves a fresh taste in your mouth, making it a great way to conclude a nice meal.

| | |
|---|---|
| 1 (12-ounce) can evaporated milk | 3 tablespoons lemon juice |
| 1 cup sugar | |

Chill the evaporated milk in the refrigerator for at least 3 hours, or overnight.

In a bowl, beat the evaporated milk until smooth and tripled in volume. Slowly add the sugar while beating.

Add the lemon juice little by little, until the mixture thickens.

Pour the mixture into an ice cream maker and process according to the manufacturer's instructions.

MY MOTHER'S BOLIVIAN KITCHEN

# Apple Flan

The rich apple flavor of this dessert makes a good finish to a nice meal.

| | |
|---|---|
| 8 green apples, such as Granny Smith, peeled and cored | 1½ cups evaporated milk |
| ¾ cups sugar | 4 eggs |

Preheat the oven to 350°F.

Place the apples in a baking pan and bake in the oven for 10–15 minutes, until soft. Puree the apples in a blender or food processor. You will need 1¼ cups of apple puree.

In a small saucepan, cook ½ cup of the sugar over low heat, stirring with a wooden spoon, until it melts and begins to caramelize. Immediately, spread the caramel in the bottom of an 8-inch baking dish.

**189**

In a bowl, beat the eggs well. Then, add the remaining ¼ cup of sugar, the evaporated milk, and 1¼ cups of the apple purée. Mix well and place in the caramel-lined baking dish.

Put the baking dish inside a larger one filled with water. Bake for 40 minutes. Check for doneness by inserting a knife into the center of the flan. If the knife comes out clean, it is ready.

# Apple Fritters

The rich apple flavor of these *buñuelos* makes them a good snack to have with tea or by themselves.

| | |
|---|---|
| 3 apples, peeled and cored | 1 egg |
| 4 teaspoons sugar | ½ cup evaporated milk |
| 2 cups flour | ½ cup vegetable oil |
| 2 teaspoons baking powder | ½ cup raisins |
| ½ teaspoon salt | |

Preheat the oven to 350°F. Fill each apple with 1 teaspoon of sugar and a little water, and bake for 15 minutes, until soft.

In a bowl, combine the flour, baking powder, salt, egg, evaporated milk, and the remaining 1 teaspoon of sugar. Mash the apples and add them to the mixture.

**190**

Heat the oil in a pan over medium heat, and fry spoonfuls of the apple mixture for 5–10 minutes.

Serve with raisins sprinkled on top.

# Bananas with Evaporated Milk

*Plátanos con Leche Evaporada*                                      6 servings

My sister Guichy used to make this sweet and sour dessert on Sundays.

| | |
|---|---|
| 2 (12-ounce) cans evaporated milk | ¼ cup sugar |
| Juice of 3 lemons | 6 bananas |

Pour the evaporated milk into a medium-size bowl and add the sugar. Beat until smooth and tripled in volume. Add the lemon juice little by little, until the mixture thickens.

Slice the bananas and distribute evenly among 6 bowls. Pour the milk mixture over the banana slices. Chill in the refrigerator for about 30 minutes. This dessert must be eaten the same day it is prepared.

# Sweet Banana Squash Fritters

*Buñuelos de Zapallo*                                      **4 servings**

Banana squash gives these crispy *buñuelos* a very different taste from those made during Christmastime.

| | |
|---|---|
| 1 cup boiled, diced banana squash | 5 teaspoons flour |
| ½ teaspoon baking powder | ¼ teaspoon salt |
| ½ cup evaporated milk | ½ cup vegetable oil |

In a bowl, combine the squash, baking powder, milk, flour, and salt. Form the mixture into patties, ½-inch-thick and 2 inches in diameter.

**192**  Heat the oil in a pan over medium heat, and fry the pastries for 10–15 minutes, or until golden brown on both sides.

# Beet Gelatin

Whenever my mother used beets, I knew she would make this dessert. She usually made it at night, placing it in the refrigerator for the next day. I loved its cinnamon taste with a touch of lemon.

| | |
|---|---|
| 5 beets, peeled | 2 teaspoons lemon juice |
| 4 cinnamon sticks | 1 envelope (1 scant teaspoon) |
| 2 teaspoons whole cloves | unflavored gelatin |

In a pot of boiling water, cook the beets with the cinnamon and cloves until the beets are tender. Remove and set aside for salad.

Quickly add the gelatin to the water used to cook the beets, and stir to mix well. Add the lemon juice and mix well.

**193**

Pour the gelatin into 6 serving bowls and refrigerate for 12 hours before serving.

# Corn Pudding

Every time I visited my family in Bolivia, I would ask my mother to make this dish for me. While she made it, we talked about many topics from food to family.

| | |
|---|---|
| 3½ cups dried white corn | 3 cinnamon sticks |
| 4 whole cloves | 1 cup sugar |

Soak the corn in plenty of cold water for 5 minutes, removing and discarding any pieces of corn that float to the surface, then drain.

In a food processor, process the corn briefly to crack the kernels.

In a large bowl, combine 3 quarts water and the corn. Stir well with a wooden spoon. Again, remove and discard any pieces of corn that float to the surface.

Slowly strain the corn through a sieve, reserving the liquid. Allow the liquid to sit for a moment. Some of the corn starch will settle. Without stirring pour the liquid into a pot, reserving the corn starch that remains in the bowl. Add the cloves and the cinnamon to the liquid in the pot. Cook over medium heat for 7 minutes. Add the corn left in the sieve. Cook for 1 hour, until the kernels burst.

Add the cornstarch that has settled in the bowl, little by little, stirring gently until dissolved. Add the sugar and cook for 20 more minutes, stirring with a wooden spoon.

Serve hot with evaporated milk, or cold with honey or molasses.

194

# Peanut Drink

The strong peanut taste, along with the cinnamon scent of this cold drink, make it a favorite that can be served anytime of the year.

| | |
|---|---|
| 1 pound peanuts, toasted | 2 cups sugar |
| ½ cup almonds | 2 pounds quinoa |
| ½ cup grated unsweetened coconut | 3 tablespoons ground cinnamon |
| 1 cup uncooked white rice | |

In a food processor, process the peanuts, almonds, coconut, and rice until finely ground. Add a few drops of water, as necessary to facilitate the grinding. Set aside.

In a pot over medium heat, combine the sugar with ½ cup water and bring to a boil. Stir to dissolve. Add the peanut mixture. Simmer, stirring for 1½ hours, or until a dry paste forms. Remove from the heat and set aside. When it is cool, place it in the refrigerator.

195

Bring 2 gallons water to a boil with the quinoa. Cook until the quinoa bursts, about 1 hour. Transfer the quinoa and the liquid to a ceramic pot and leave it to ferment for 2 days at room temperature.

In a big container, strain and discard the quinoa. Stir the peanut mixture into the quinoa liquid, little by little, making sure it is well mixed with the quinoa water. Add sugar to taste, and serve cold with ¼ teaspoon ground cinnamon per glass sprinkled on top.

**Note:** This drink needs to be consumed the day it is made. Leftover peanut drink becomes thick and does not taste as good.

# Quince Jelly

This jelly was made by my mother and my sister Guichy. As a child, I always thought that it took them too long to make it. I guess that was because once the jelly was made, we had to wait until the next day to eat it because it needed to set. It was offered at tea time to spread on bread.

2 pounds quinces
2 cups sugar (approximately)

Wash the quinces well and rub the fuzz off with a cloth. Quarter each quince, leaving the seeds and skin.

Boil the quince in water to cover until very tender. Line a sieve with cheesecloth. Turn the quince into the cheesecloth and let drain overnight into a bowl. Discard the liquid.

196

Pass the pulp through a sieve, discarding the seeds and skin. Weigh the pulp and place it in a pot. Add an equal amount of sugar and cook, stirring with a wooden spoon, until the sugar is dissolved. Boil rapidly until the mixture gets thick and clear enough that you can see the bottom of the pan.

Remove the jelly from the heat and pour into hot sterile jars. Cover with lids and store in a cool place.

The jelly keeps for a couple of weeks refrigerated.

# Sweet Quinoa Patties

*Buñuelos* are usually associated with Christmas, but this type can be made any time of the year and served as an appetizer.

| | |
|---|---|
| ¼ cup quinoa (see Note) | 1 teaspoon baking powder |
| 1 teaspoon salt | 1 teaspoon ground cinnamon |
| 1 cup evaporated milk | 3 egg whites, lightly beaten |
| 1 tablespoon sugar | ½ cup vegetable oil |
| 1 cup flour | |

In a pot over medium heat, bring 2 cups of water to a boil. Add the quinoa and salt and boil for 10 minutes. Reduce the heat to simmer and cook for 45 minutes, until the quinoa bursts. Add the evaporated milk and cook for an additional 10–15 minutes. Remove from the heat and set aside to cool.

Add the sugar, flour, baking powder, salt, cinnamon, and egg whites.

Form the mixture into patties, ¼-inch thick and 2-inches in diameter.

Heat the oil in a pan over medium heat, and fry the patties for 10–15 minutes, or until golden brown on both sides.

**Note:** If you bought the quinoa from a health food store, you probably got it in a box pretty much ready to be used. However, if you got the quinoa from a farmers' market, you need to wash it thoroughly, in sufficient water, 3–4 times, making sure is free of any other little particles.

It is important to remember that salt should never be added when you are cooking any type of dish with quinoa. Use salt only after the quinoa is cooked; otherwise the quinoa won't cook well.

197

# Rice Pudding

This recipe, although more of a dessert, was sometimes served in a big bowl as dinner. The sweet taste of milk and cinnamon served warm, was truly appealing to my sisters and me.

| | |
|---|---|
| 1 cup white rice | 4 tablespoons sugar, or to taste |
| 2 cinnamon sticks | ½ teaspoon ground cinnamon |
| 2 cups evaporated milk | |

In a large pot, bring 3½ cups water to a boil, add the rice and cinnamon sticks, and cook for 5 minutes. Reduce the heat to a simmer and continue cooking for 20 minutes, stirring occasionally with a wooden spoon.

Add the evaporated milk and the sugar, and cook an additional 15 minutes, stirring. Remove from heat.

**198**

Serve hot or cold, with ground cinnamon sprinkled on top.

# Egg Custard

The sweet taste of this cold dessert is appealing after a good dinner.

| | |
|---|---|
| 12 eggs | 2 cups sugar |
| 4 cups milk | |

Preheat the oven to 350°F.

Beat the eggs well in a large bowl, then, add the milk and sugar.

Pour the mixture into a 2-quart baking dish and bake for approximately 1 hour. Check for doneness by inserting a knife deep into the center. If the knife comes out clean, it is ready.

Serve chilled.

**199**

# Rum Omelet

This is a sweet, eggy dessert with a taste of rum.

| | |
|---|---|
| 8 eggs, lightly beaten | ½ cup rum |
| ¼ cup evaporated milk | 1 tablespoon vegetable oil |
| 2 tablespoons sugar | |

In a bowl, combine the eggs and milk.

Heat the oil in a pan over medium heat, and add the egg mixture. Reduce the heat and simmer for 5–10 minutes.

Sprinkle 1 teaspoon of the sugar evenly over the egg mixture. Remove the omelet from the heat and set aside on a heatproof pan. Roll up the tortilla and sprinkle with the rest of the sugar.

**200**

In a small pot over medium heat, heat the rum until hot. Sprinkle a little of the rum evenly over the omelet. Use a match to set fire to it. Pour the remaining rum over the omelet.

Serve hot.

# Tangerine Dessert

The refreshing tangerine taste of this dessert is good after lunch, particularly on a hot day.

| | |
|---|---|
| 1 envelope unflavored gelatin | Sugar to taste |
| 2 cups boiling water | 2 egg whites |
| 6 cups tangerine juice | |

In a bowl, dissolve the gelatin in the boiling water. Add the juice and sugar. Place in the refrigerator for 15 minutes until it thickens a little. Beat the egg whites until stiff peaks form. Fold the egg whites into the tangerine mixture. Chill the dessert in the refrigerator for a few hours until set.

201

# Sweet Yucca Patties

For all those yucca lovers wanting to find an excuse to eat more yucca, this pastry is a good reason.

| | |
|---|---|
| 2 pounds yucca | 2 tablespoons flour |
| 1 teaspoon salt | 1½ cups strawberry jam |
| 1 tablespoon sugar | 1 egg white |
| 1 teaspoon ground cinnamon | ½ cup olive oil |

Peel the yucca and slice it into 3-inch pieces. Halve the slices, and remove and discard the core.

Bring 8 cups water to a boil in a large pot, add the yucca and 1 teaspoon of the salt. Boil the yucca for 20 minutes, until almost tender. Drain and set aside. Do not overcook or it will become mushy and fall apart.

**202**

In a bowl, combine the yucca, sugar, cinnamon, and flour. Mix well and knead until soft and smooth. Divide the mixture into pieces the size of a tennis ball.

Enclose 1 teaspoon of jam in the middle of each ball and flatten the dough into 1-inch thick, 3-inch diameter patties.

In a bowl, beat the egg white with 1 tablespoon water, and brush over the patties.

Heat the oil in a flat-bottomed pan over medium heat, and fry the patties until golden brown on both sides.

# AFTERWORD

In Spanish, *añoranza* means "nostalgia." Like most Spanish words, it also embraces other meanings, such as a sense of loss. In trying to describe the feelings I had when I lost my mother, there were times this word defined my emotions, and it became a kind of mantra I could repeat when I felt a need to release *añoranzas*.

The last time I saw my mother alive was in 1998 at the Cochabamba airport as my wife Tina and I were returning to the U.S. after spending the holidays there. I walked through the airport checkpoints, my clothes still impregnated with the embraces from all my family there to see me off—sisters, nephews, nieces, my brothers-in-law and my mother. It was the first time in my life that I felt the need for another embrace from her before leaving. My wife, the passengers behind me, and the airline workers witnessed my sudden change of behavior as I made my way back in the opposite direction from where I was going. I was in front of my family again, who were surprised and did not have time to ask why I was there rather than on the plane. The answer was in front of them as I embraced my mother a second time without knowing or understanding why I had that impulse. I never imagined it would be the last time I saw her and that this embrace would be the last we would ever share.

Following the shock of her death, I buried myself in my work, unable to handle the pain knocking at my heart. I didn't want to answer its call. Only my work routine distracted me from my emotions. It seemed as if work could numb my grief. When summer came, I had more time to myself, without the everyday demands of teaching. It was then that pain rushed in like water coming down from a mountain, and I had to deal with it.

Tina, who is a writer, suggested that, as a form of therapy, I should write down some of the stories I had told her about my childhood. When I began writing these memoirs, the flood of memories and images of my mother imprinted themselves on my dreams. From that torrent of dream images, one in particular stands out: I was in a big valley with a golden-yellow wheat field. The wheat reached my knees. I saw my mother walking toward me, wearing a green wool sweater she'd had. She looked peaceful but I could sense the sadness in her eyes when she expressed how sorry she was that her death caused me pain. I couldn't talk because tears flooded inside me. Then I felt her embrace as she told me she was there to say good-bye. As she walked away from me, I felt my heart pumping like a horse running wild, but afterward a sense of peace settled upon me.

The memory of my mother remains strong in my heart. I learned to understand how, when she cooked for people, she felt the joy of making them feel cared for. I now experience this feeling when I make meals for family and friends. There is something joyful about sitting with someone at a table to share the food you prepared.

Writing this book became a healing experience. I hope you will venture into making Bolivian dishes for your loved ones, or for yourself, and in doing so will taste its pleasures.

# RESOURCES

## BOOKS

Club. "La Orquidea." *El Placer de Comer*. Cochabamba: Editorial Los Amigos del Libro, 1986.

Davidson, Alan. *The Oxford Companion of Food*. Oxford: Oxford University Press, 1999.

de Jordán, Nelly. *Nuestras Comidas*. Cochabamba: Federación Nacional de Cooperativas de Ahorro y Crédito de Bolivia, 1997.

*Encylopedia Britannica 2004 Book of the Year*. "Bolivia." Chicago: Encyclopedia Britannica, Inc., 2004.

Mesa Gisbert, Carlos D. *Historia de Bolivia*. La Paz: Don Bosco Press, 1997.

Novas, Himilce and Rosemary Silva. ed. *Latin American Cooking Across the U. S.* New York: Alfred A. Knopf, Inc., 1997.

Putnam, Giselle. *Cocina Típica Boliviana*. La Paz: IMBOLEC S.R.L., 1998.

Sánchez-H., José. *The Art and Politics of Bolivian Cinema*. Maryland: Scarecrow Press, Inc., 1999.

Swaaney, Deanna and Robert Strauss. *Bolivia: A Travel Survival Kit*. Hawthorn: Lonely Planet Publications, 1992.

## ARTICLES

"Bolivia Gets New Chief After Protests," *Press Telegram* (Long Beach), 18 October 2003, A-18.

205

"Bolivian Leader Promises Elections," *Los Angeles Times* (Los Angeles), 19 October 2003, A-4.

Fundación PROINPA, "Cultivos Nativos Bolivianos, Riqueza Genética Para la Humanidad," LAB (Bolivia) 26, no. 6, November-December 2002.

Tobar, Hector. "Across the Americas, Indigenous Peoples Make Themselves Heard," *Los Angeles Times* (Los Angeles), 19 December 2003, A-1, A-4.

"Bolivian President Exits Amid Uprising," *Los Angeles Times* (Los Angeles), 18 December 2003, 1, 9.

## INTERNET

www.boliviamall.com

www.boliviaweb.com

www.explorebolivia.com

206

# INDEX

207

211

212

eggs

All Saints' Sweet Bread
(*Bizcocho de Todos Santos*),
170

Apple Flan (*Flan de Manzanas*),
189

Baked Breaded Steak (*Asado en
Leche*), 128

Baked Macaroni Casserole (*Pastel
de Macarones al Horno*), 44

Baked Rice Casserole (*Pastel de
Arroz al Horno*), 45

Baked Rice Soup (*Sopa de Arroz
al Horno*), 74

Beef with *Chuño* (*Ch'ajchu*),
122–123

Beef with Fried Eggs (*Lomo
Montado*), 120–121

Breaded Beef Cutlets
(*Sillp'anchu*), 127

Bread Soup (*Sopa de Pan*), 61

Cheese, Chili, and Onion
Turnovers (*Empanadas
Pukas*), 160–161

Cheese Omelet (*Tortilla de
Huevos con Queso*), 43

Chicken Salad (*Salpicón*), 92

Chicken with Carrots (*Pollo a la
"Señorita"*), 85

Christmas Doughnuts (*Buñuelos
de Navidad*), 173

Christmas Turnovers with
Cheese (*Pasteles Navideños
con Queso*), 157

Cinnamon Rolls (*Rollos de
Canela*), 172

Cochabamba Empanadas
(*Empanadas Cochabambinas*),
164

Condensed Milk Cake (*Queque
con Leche Condensada*), 174

eggs (continued)

Corn Pastry with Chicken
Stuffing (*Pastel de Choclo con
Relleno de Pollo*), 102–103

Creole Pork Roll (*Enrollado
Criollo*), 138

Egg Custard (*Leche Asada*), 199

Fried Chicken with Cream
(*Pollo Frito en Crema*), 95

Holy Week Sweet Bread
(*Bizcocho de Semana Santa*),
178–179

Meat Pies (*Salteñas*), 162–163

Meat-Stuffed Chicken (*Pollo
Relleno de Carnes*), 98

Milk Ice Cream (*Helado de
Leche*), 187

Nut Cake (*Queque de Nuez*), 175

Potato Casserole (*Pastel de
Papas al Horno*), 37

Quinoa Fritters (*Bocadillos de
Quinua*), 48

Quinoa Stew (*P'isque de
Quinua*), 49

Rum Omelet (*Tortilla con Ron*),
200

Sautéed Freeze-Dried Potatoes
(*Chuño Phuti*), 34

Sponge Cake (*Bizcochuelo*), 177

Stuffed Christmas Turnovers
(*Pasteles Navideños con
Relleno*), 158–159

Stuffed Potato Balls (*Relleno de
Papas*), 38–39

Stuffed Rice Soup (*Sopa de
Arroz Rellena*), 75

Sun-Dried Beef with Rice
(*Majao*), 116–117

214

215

216

217

219

221

224

225